Criminal Justice
Recent Scholarship

Edited by
Marilyn McShane and Frank P. Williams III

A Series from LFB Scholarly

Building a Culture of Lawfulness
Law Enforcement, Legal Reasoning, and Delinquency among Mexican Youth

Heath B. Grant

LFB Scholarly Publishing LLC
New York 2006

Library of Congress Cataloging-in-Publication Data

Grant, Heath B.
  Building a culture of lawfulness : law enforcement, legal reasoning,
and delinquency among Mexican youth / Heath B. Grant.
    p. cm. -- (Criminal justice recent scholarship)
  Includes bibliographical references and index.
  ISBN 1-59332-138-4 (alk. paper)
  1. Juvenile delinquency--Prevention. 2. Juvenile delinquency--
Mexico. 3. Youth--Mexico--Attitudes. 4. Criminal justice,
Administration of--Mexico--Public opinion. 5. Law enforcement--
Mexico--Public opinion. I. Title. II. Series: Criminal justice (LFB
Scholarly Publishing LLC)
  HV9076.5.G69 2006
  364.360972--dc22

    2006014609

ISBN 1-59332-138-4

Printed on acid-free 250-year-life paper.

Manufactured in the United States of America.

Table of Contents

List of Figures

List of Tables

Acknowledgements

Foremost, I need to thank Dr. Dennis Kenney for not only introducing me to the Culture of Lawfulness Project at the National Strategy Information Center (NSIC), from which this study was born, but also because Dennis has played both a supportive and demanding role throughout my career to date. To him, I will always be grateful for putting me on a path that pulled together much of my previous work in a way that will remain my direction for years to come.

Participating in the training and evaluation of the Culture of Lawfulness project throughout Latin America has been an incredible experience, especially, seeing the program grow from one state in Mexico to now truly being a global presence reaching hundreds of thousands of youths globally. This project also required me learning another language in addition to Spanish: structural equation modeling. Despite the daunting nature of these statistics, Dr. Keith Markus was able to talk me through the learning process with ease, always being available and critical where necessary. Dr. Charles Bahn has been a source of inspiration for me from the early days of my research, and has always pushed me to move towards career advancement. I am lucky to have benefited from his influence throughout this process.

Anyone reading the manuscript that follows must know that it also would not be possible but for the support and guidance of NSIC. Not only did they provide the extremely rich data that makes up this book, but they have allowed me to participate in a central role in the training, evaluation, and development of this incredible worldwide effort.

Special mention must be made to the inspiration of Dr. Roy Godson, the president of NSIC that had the vision to develop a school-based (and ultimately system-wide effort) that forms the basis of this work. The Culture of Lawfulness Program continues to expand based upon his continued dedication and efforts. The influence of NSIC Executive Director, Jeff Berman, in always challenging and re-articulating the ideas found in this book must also be stressed. Expressing thanks to NSIC will never be enough. I am proud to be a part of this amazing effort.

At the risk of sounding trite, I have also been blessed with a family that has unconditionally accepted my decisions and supported me in every stage of this process. Few people are lucky enough to have the backing of parents such as Carole and Garry Grant. My other brothers Scott, Geoff, and Mike will always be respected for their guidance and love. I must mention the many friends that have always been there for me: Jennifer Davies, Adriana Kicornick – Mina, Mark Bernard, Rene Goodstein, Karen Terry, Krister Kottmeir, Kevin O'Toole, Cathryn Lavery, Nicole Robbins, Susan Winton and Regina Moroney. Thanks to each of you for the support you have always given me.

Last, but certainly not least, my doctoral student Sheetal Ranjan deserves more than special mention. It is a blessing for a professor when a solid student comes along that can help manifest your work at a time when you have no time yourself. Sheetal is responsible for the entire editing process of this book when I was consumed with work on my newest project as Director of Research and Global Training for the Spirituality for Kids Foundation.

I have been particularly blessed with being able to transfer the knowledge and skills gained over the years with the Culture of Lawfulness program to another global effort that is transforming the lives of kids and their families everywhere. To this end, I would like to personally thank the Rav and Karen Berg for their global vision and the personal impact it has had in my own life. Yehuda and Michal Berg, Sarah Yardeni, Rachel Stone, Philippe Van den Bossche, and everyone a part of the global SFK family, thank you for supporting me on this path that will continue to foster youth resiliency everywhere.

Heath Grant

CHAPTER ONE

The Research Problem

<u>Introduction</u>

The objective of the current study is to assess the application of the theory of legal socialization to resiliency theory, explaining the extent to which legal reasoning mediates between the criminogenic influences of selected community and individual risk factors.

By examining the causal pathways and relationships between risk/protective factors, legal reasoning, perceptions of legitimacy, and behavior, the current study offers an integrative approach that bridges much of the current thoughts and findings in the criminological literature. The study seeks to build upon important findings in the field of legal socialization (Cohn and White, 1990; Finckenauer, 1995; Jones Brown, 1996), offering explanation as to the degree to which legal reasoning is affected by legal culture, in addition to other variables commonly cited in the research literature such as having delinquent peers; exposure to gangs and violence; low school attachment; low self-esteem; and, having an external locus of control.

<u>Theoretical Bases of the Study: Legal Culture and Legal Socialization</u>

Legal socialization refers to the "development of values, attitudes, and behaviors toward law" (Finckenauer, 1995). Growing out of the cognitive developmental paradigm it focuses principally upon "the

1

individual's standards for making sociolegal judgements and for resolving conflicts, pressing claims, and settling disputes" (Tapp and Levine, 1974, pg.4). According to this paradigm, legal reasoning develops across three levels throughout the life-course consistent with Kohlberg's moral reasoning theory: from a preconventional law-obeying desire to obey the law in fear of punishment, to a conventional law-maintaining individual's need to conform to informal and formal groups in society, to finally the postconventional lawmaking emphasis on ethics and morality when assessing the need for compliance with rules and laws (Tapp and Kohlberg, 1977). These levels also mirror the general cognitive development of a child outlined in the work of Piaget (1932). More completely, there are a series of stages within the three levels in which an individual progresses from law compliance "because they will be punished if they do not (stage 1), or to please others (stage 2), or out of blind obedience to the law (stages 3 and 4) – they should......ideally.....be lawful because they are concerned with the social quality of their communities (stage 5) and because they respect others, even those unlike themselves (stage 6)" (Gardiner, pg.10).[1]

The three levels of reasoning reflect the maturation of moral and legal reasoning, operating as cognitive structures rather than beliefs about the world, providing 'ways of organizing information" (Jones-Brown, 1996, pg. 35) as the individual interacts within the situational and environmental context. Higher levels of reasoning are said to be associated with less delinquency. Cohn and White (1990) note that cross-cultural data suggests that while individuals sometimes reason below their cognitive stage, most do not reason above unless in a transitional phase.

Although the cognitive developmental perspective emphasizes such internal information-processing structures as ultimately influencing one's probability of engaging in law-aiding behaviors, there is also the recognition of the "potential for environmental factors to

---

[1] Much greater analysis and discussion of cognitive development and legal socialization theories will be provided throughout Chapters Two and Three. The discussion here is meant only to provide the reader with a brief overview of the research problem.

retard or accelerate the development of moral and legal reasoning" (Jones-Brown, pg. 42), making it a useful vantage point from which to examine, and ultimately explain, resiliency within high-risk environments. Such factors can include the peer, family, and social pressures already found to play important roles in predicting delinquency. Thus, arguably legal reasoning could be an explanatory variable accounting for why some individuals coming from the same balance of risk and protective factors ultimately end up involved in criminal activity.

Moreover, the legal socialization literature also recognizes the reciprocal relationship that legal contexts can play in shaping how youths think and behave in relationship to the law (Finckenauer, 1995). Societies functioning in the absence of a rule of law, where corruption, brutality, and inequality characterize the average citizen's interaction with the legal institutions and law enforcement (Marshall, 1977), may thus be contributing to increasing lawlessness on the part of the average citizen through the mechanism of legal reasoning. Social factors can produce the level of moral reasoning that subsequently results in delinquency (Morash, 1983).

The rule-enforcing environment, or legal context, can include such factors as the fair enforcement of rules, the legitimacy of rules, and the role of authority. Cohn and White (1990) varied the legal context in their study of legal socialization on a university campus, by creating two dramatically different environments for study participants. In the external authority condition, residents had no control over rule enforcement. Moreover, rules were strictly enforced by the residence director, with no discretionary flexibility to account for case-by-case variation. In contrast, other students were placed in a peer community condition in which the students themselves operated the internal disciplinary hearing board, electing representatives on behalf of the larger residence community. Although the effect was small, rule violation across the study period was greater in the external authority condition, where students were more likely to develop attitudes against the rules themselves, as well as their enforcement.

Voluntary compliance with the law may thus be tied into the degree to which the criminal justice system and its respective components are viewed as legitimate and deserving of compliance

(Tyler, 1990). The belief that teachers and authorities treat students fairly has been identified as a significant resiliency variable in some studies (McKnight and Loper, 2002). Moreover, the importance of future research emphasizing the connections between the resiliency and legal socialization literature is also hinted at by findings that resilient boys appear to come from households and schools where there is greater structure, rules and both parental and teacher supervision (Wallerstein and Kelly, 1979).

Rawls (1971) offers the causal chain described in Figure-1 that will frame the central research objectives of this study:

Figure 1 Rawls Causal Chain

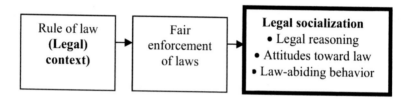

The current study will examine the relationship between selected community and individual risk factors (i.e. personal safety, delinquent peers, locus of control, school attachment, self-esteem), legitimacy factors such as perceptions of law enforcement fairness and obligation to obey the law, social responsibility, and legal socialization (legal reasoning; attitudes toward law-obligation/social responsibility; behavior). Additionally, through the use of structural equation modeling (SEM), the researcher will be able to examine the degree to which perceptions of police fairness and selected risk factors influence legal reasoning, which in turn influences perceived obligation to obey the law, and ultimately law-abiding behavior. Although the construct of legal and moral reasoning as resiliency has been suggested for years, no empirical work of this nature has examined the pathway between the social factors and legal reasoning that is said to lead to conforming behavior, beyond establishing relationships between constructs as described below. Morash (1983) points to the need for such research twenty years ago:

Although Kohlberg's work (1984) opened the door for considering moral structure as an insulation from the pressures to be delinquent, it did not adequately specify the factors against which insulation is needed, and it did not demonstrate the effectiveness of the insulation (pg. 390).

Implications of the Current Study

The recognition that legitimacy of law enforcement might actually influence the development of legal reasoning demonstrates the need to build mechanisms of reform in criminal justice institutions that move towards a rule of law society. Thus, technical assistance to developing countries or countries in transition will have an empirical impetus for improving police-community interaction, or the fairness of legislative practices, in order to truly build a society that lives within a culture of lawfulness.

Throughout the world, crime and corruption pose serious problems that challenge the overall functioning of democratic societies, or those "transitioning" towards democracy. Moreover, although the commonly cited correlation between poverty and crime in Third World or developing countries is often used as evidence for explaining the existence of crime, the reverse effect of continued economic decline with the presence of crime and disorder is also a well-documented trend (Wilson and Kelling, 1982; Orlando, 2001). However, while the recognition that law enforcement has an important function in combating the presence of crime and disorder is readily acknowledged, the limitations of such approaches to crime reduction are often overlooked.

Godson (2000) notes that while the suppressive techniques of traditional law enforcement are a necessary approach to combating crime and corruption, particularly where organized crime is involved, they are not sufficient. He argues that a complementary strategy is also needed, amounting to a fundamental shift in values; or in other words, he is referring to a society or culture that is sympathetic to the rule of law.

Bolstered by a sympathetic culture – a culture of lawfulness – law enforcement and regulatory systems function more effectively in myriad ways. Those who transgress the rules find themselves targeted not only by law enforcement but also by many sectors of society. Community support and involvement can also focus on preventing and on rooting out criminal and corrupt practices without the need for expenditures for a massive law enforcement and punitive establishment. This involvement also reduces the risk and expense of intrusive government surveillance and regulatory practices harmful to individual liberties and creative economic, social, and political initiatives. In other words, law enforcement is but one wheel of a two-wheeled coach (Godson, 2000).

Crime is caused by established factors such as poverty, disorder, and the numerous other variables noted in the criminological literature; however, it is argued that there is a significant proportion of its variance that remains unexplained. In addition to the socioeconomic factors commonly advanced, there is an important role for civic society. Even in the poorest, crime ridden neighborhoods, the majority of citizens are not involved in criminality. The challenge for governments and international criminal justice policy-makers thus involves fostering a citizenry that is unwilling to participate in criminal activities, and intolerant of its existence in their schools, communities, or countries.

The current study examines one of the factors hypothesized to be a key ingredient in insulating an individual against criminality, despite high risk situations. On a societal scale, a culture of lawfulness is expected to be facilitated in areas in which the majority of people are reasoning on a post-conventional level. The sympathetic culture that Godson (2000) speaks of involves citizens complying with the law based upon conviction in the principals of justice and fairness inherent in the rule of law ideal (level three), rather than out of a fear of punishment (level one) or need for conformity (level two).

It is expected that an individual's advancement in legal reasoning levels is correlated with a greater support for the rule of law, and is facilitated by the presence of fair and effective law enforcement on the macro level. One can expect that in societies that rely on repressive law enforcement tactics and punishment to instill compliance (or where practices are corrupt and brutal) legal values will be diverse – with fewer individuals appreciating the moral validity of the law, or principles thought to be inherent in the rule of law, such as equality, openness, and justice (Cohn and White, 1997). It may be the case that in such societies there is even a lesser knowledge of the law. In contrast, where government has legitimacy and there exists a strong sense of both political and social rights, one can expect a higher level of legal reasoning, characterized by the greater sense of social responsibility common to post-conventional thinkers. Each of these issues will be fleshed out further in the following chapter. To summarize; without this larger sense of legitimacy, individuals may be less inclined to appreciate the inherent moral value of the law and legal processes, thereby causing the state to rely on more coercive practices common to police states to enforce compliance (Finckenauer, 1995).

This is particularly relevant given the recent findings of the International Crime (Victim) Survey (ICVS) that in developing countries and countries in transition towards democracy, the majority of respondents showed a marked lack of confidence in law enforcement capacities, capabilities, and even willingness to serve the community (Zvekic, 1998). This finding manifests itself in terms of a decreased willingness to report crime or victimization to the police, as well as overall evaluations of satisfaction.

One intervention that directly targets the development of legal reasoning and perceptions of the legitimacy of police and the criminal justice system is law-related education programs. Such programs, particularly popular during the early 1980's, sought to help students appreciate the "Rousseauian" principles of social contract that in order to have certain rights, people must exercise responsibility and respect for the rights. A two year OJJDP sponsored research study of such efforts in six communities throughout the United States found that students were better able to solve problems and refrain from delinquency following participation in law-related education (LRE Project Exchange, 1982).

Greenberg and Wertlieb (1985) report similar successes in a study of 1,054 elementary, junior high, and senior high school students participating in law-related education in five states. Students were less likely than comparisons to engage in 8 of 10 measured delinquent behaviors, in addition to showing improvements in many factors associated with law-abiding behavior. Chorak (1997) relates the success of properly implemented law-related education programs to the development of social competence and cognitive problem-solving skills commonly cited in the resiliency literature. The current study will be the first large-scale empirical effort to examine the causal path between the cognitive element of legal reasoning and commonly cited predictors such as community safety, attitudes towards police, delinquent peers, as well as important factors related to youth sense of autonomy, such as self-esteem and locus of control.

By looking at these factors within a causal pathway, the findings of the current research will provide meaningful information to practitioners seeking to develop or improve law-related education programs. An empirical base will be provided for the first time as to which factors are important to address in law-related programming. Later replications in other countries will also examine the transferability of these findings, and thus such programming, across international boundaries.

Finally, there is a conflicting body of literature related to the importance of knowledge of the law in promoting higher levels of legal reasoning. Greater knowledge of the law leading to positive attitudes towards the law and consequently law-abiding behavior has been reported in some efforts (Law-Related Education, 1983; Zimmer and Huston, 1987), but completely unrelated in others (Rafky and Sealey, 1975; Jacobson and Palonsky, 1981; Markowitz, 1986). Although the current study is cross-sectional in that it only uses the pre-test data, later work combining the post-test results can examine the degree to which exposure to law-related education impacts the pathways revealed in this effort.

Selecting the Target Area and Population: examining legal culture and socialization amongst Mexican youths
------

The current study is unprecedented in the field of legal socialization in terms of its tremendous sample size of over 10,000 respondents; this fact alone promises to offer a significant contribution to the literature. Moreover, the attachment of this study to a larger project involving many countries around the world with different legal contexts (including the United States), allows for future replications to examine the cross-cultural applicability of the pathways derived empirically in this dissertation.

Based upon the successes of school-based programming to help prevent crime and corruption in Palermo, Sicily and Hong Kong, the Ministry of Education of Baja California, Mexico, and the San Diego County Office of Education (Sweetwater District) brought together teachers and education specialists from both sides of the border to develop and implement a pilot curriculum to increase children's knowledge of crime and corruption, as well as strengthen their support for the rule of law and a culture of lawfulness.

An evaluation of the pilot curriculum after its first year involving anonymous testing of over 800 students revealed that the project improved student's knowledge of and resistance to crime, as well as interpersonal capacities, such as self-esteem, and problem-solving (Godson and Kenney, 2000). The theoretical foundations for this program and its connections to the variables being measured in the current study will be detailed in chapter 4 following a more thorough examination of the key theoretical concepts discussed throughout this chapter. Following the success of the first year, the curriculum was revised and expanded to schools throughout the entire country of Mexico, and its implementation and testing is now well underway in countries as diverse as the former Soviet Republic of Georgia, Columbia, Peru, and El Salvador.

In the fall of 2001, a large-scale second evaluation was conducted across the state of Baja, California to examine the sustainability of outcomes following the expansion of the program beyond the original four pilot sites in Tijuana (compared to 4 comparison schools) and revisions to the curriculum. In this effort, 10,437 youths were anonymously pre-tested within their school settings prior to beginning the Baja California Culture of Lawfulness curriculum (NSIC, 2001).

As an evaluation consultant to the National Strategy Information Center (NSIC), the researcher of this study was asked to select theoretically-derived scales[2] to support the measurement of pre-post changes in the knowledge, attitudes, and behaviors of the students participating in the program in *secundarias* (i.e. middle schools) throughout Baja California. The same instrument is being used as the project expands throughout the world, with constant attention to re-validation in new cultural contexts. Future research will build on this effort with cross-cultural comparisons of the current study's findings.

Although there are not a great deal of cross-cultural studies of legal socialization, the largest such work began in a cross-national 1965 study of Denmark, Greece, India, Italy, Japan, and the United States (Hess and Tapp, 1969; Minturn and Tapp, 1970; Tapp, 1970). In addition, work examining the cultural universality of Kohlberg's stages of moral development with middle and lower class urban boys, as well as illiterate villagers in Mexico, Taiwan, Turkey, and the United States has been conducted (Kohlberg, 1968; Kohlberg and Turiel, 1971; Tapp and Kohlberg, 1977). Although each of these efforts provided some of the conceptual foundations for legal socialization theory, and its transferability across contexts, this work failed to empirically examine the influence of legitimacy and known risk factors on the pathway to legal reasoning development and behavior conducted in this study.

The most recent and comprehensive examination of legal socialization across comparative international legal contexts is found in Finckenauer's (1995) study of youths in the former Soviet Union, post-Glasnost Russia, and the United States. Finckenauer (1995) was able to examine the influence of these very different legal contexts on legal socialization, including the relationship between legal reasoning level and delinquency. Building on the work of other scholars in the area of legitimacy (Tyler, 1990; Tyler and Rasinski, 1991), Finckenauer's (1995) study is based on the premise that "voluntary compliance with the law issues in part from a legal order and justice system which is

---

[2] Including measures of self-esteem, personal safety, locus of control, peer associations, support for the police, fatalism, attitudes toward school, legal reasoning, legitimacy, social responsibility, and delinquency. The structure and validity of this Mexican Culture of Lawfulness instrument is detailed in chapter five.

seen to be legitimate, and is believed to be deserving of respect and compliance" (Finckenauer, pg. 6). Thus, compliance with the law can be influenced by both macro (e.g. corrupt or brutal law enforcement) and micro-level (e.g. presence of delinquent peers, neighborhood safety, school attachment) concerns (Jones Brown, 1996).

A major criticism of legal socialization research is the difficulty in sorting out the direction of influences across selected variables (Blasi, 1980; Morash, 1983; Finckenauer, 1995). For example, does legal reasoning cause behavior, or does behavior lead to legal reasoning level? As a result, this author feels that SEM provides the most descriptive possibilities in terms of understanding the nature of legal socialization as well as the impact of key contextual and individual variables on both legal reasoning and subsequent law compliance (Cohn and White, 1990).

Although the influence of variables such as external locus of control, self-esteem, and delinquent peers have been noted in previous work (Jones Brown, 1996), the current study empirically measures the degree to which these factors can either retard or accelerate legal reasoning.

Although the influence of multiple risk factors interacting across each of the domains noted above has been empirically demonstrated to contribute to belief structures contrary to formal authority, this analysis fails to account for the potential role of the macro-level legal context or culture emphasized in the political psychology or procedural justice literature. At some level micro and macro explanations should intersect for an integrated criminological theory of delinquency; this study attempts to explore such connections. The extent to which changes in perceptions of the legitimacy of authorities affect the level of compliance with the law in everyday lives is an important question, particularly where we are dealing with countries at different levels of democratization (Cohn and White, 1997).

Studying Legal Socialization in Mexico

The opportunity to study the legal socialization of Mexican youths provides an interesting context because; although on the surface it exhibits many of the conditions of democratic rule, "relations between government and society, particularly the poor and marginalized members of society, have been characterized by the illegal and arbitrary use of power" (Pinheiro, pg. 1). Although the end of one-party rule brought hopes of human rights and a rule of law society, the reality is that there remains a significant disparity "between the letter of the bill of rights, present in (the) constitution, and law enforcement application and practice" (Ibid.). Access to "justice" in many cases is bought with money, a tool more available to narcotraffickers than the average citizen.

Practices such as enforced disappearances, although decreasing significantly throughout Latin America, continue to exist in Mexico. After many such disappearances in Mexico throughout the 1970s and 1980s, the incidence of such events stayed in the single figures from 1982 to 1991, with none reported in 1992 and 1993 (Rodley, 1999). However, the Chiapas uprising showed that the practice had not disappeared, producing 37 cases in 1994 and 21 cases in 1995 (Ibid.).

As with many countries throughout Latin America, a semi-military model of policing exists in Mexico, in which police administrators see their role as fighting the "enemy" of crime regardless of the constraints on arbitrary enforcement meant to be offered by the law and the criminal justice system (Chevigny, 1999). Although decreasing, this "military ethos" has helped to maintain a legal context in which the practices of torture and use of deadly force to suppress social movements has not disappeared. The use of special squads, such as the notorious Jaguars unit formerly in the federal district, has been characterized by human rights organizations as becoming "a law unto themselves" (NSIC, 2001).

A driving force behind the above abuses and citizen perceptions of police impunity in general stems from corruption, beginning with low level bribes and extending to include protection rackets. Chevigny (1999) argues that corruption and police brutality are interrelated because "together they show the power of the police, their independence from the rest of the criminal justice system, and their ability to administer justice as they see fit" (Chevigny, 62). Paying bribes is a common practice in countries such as Mexico, not just as a means of bypassing the criminal justice system, but also to avoid retribution and physical harassment at the hands of officers for citizens who refuse to pay. This legal context will not go far in socializing youths as to the value of rules and laws and their enforcement in society[3]. The importance of this cannot be underestimated; legislation is meaningless unless the government is able to "anticipate that the citizenry as a whole will.........generally observe the body of rules promulgated" (Fuller, pg.201). Given the fact that laws are created to enforce behavior that many people would often rather avoid, legal authorities are best served "establish(ing) and maintain(ing) conditions that lead the public generally to accept their decisions and policies" (Tyler, pg.19). A government that needs to rely on coercion as a means of maintaining compliance with the law will be faced with an insurmountable task, both in terms of resource cost and practicality.

<u>Summary</u>

This chapter summarizes the major theoretical issues being addressed in the current research. Although the focus of this effort is on legal socialization, and its emphases on the relationship between the law, reasoning, attitudes, and behavior, as the literature began to be examined, the linkages between this field of study and the broader focuses of resiliency and legitimacy theory becomes apparent. As such, the need to provide an integrative theoretical framework synthesizing major findings from each of these areas is the major objective of this study.The importance of the legal context for the development of legal reasoning has been the focus of other researchers. Cohn and White (1990) studied this relationship with a quasi-experimental study of university students; Finckenauer (1995) compared the legal reasoning levels of Soviet and American youths;

---

[3] Chapter 4 will detail the legal context of Mexico further, in order to provide an adequate analytical background within which to interpret the study results.

whereas Jones Brown (1996) examined the differences in how African-American and white youths experience the law. Although the connection between changing legal contexts and an individual's level of legal reasoning has been discussed since Tapp and Kohlberg (1977), the empirical connection between legitimacy levels and stage of reasoning has not yet been explored. Thus, the central research questions of this study are[4]:

• To what degree do negative youth perceptions of the legitimacy of law enforcement impact legal reasoning level?

• What is the causal pathway between perceptions of the police, legal reasoning, and obligation to obey the law? Do legitimacy factors such as support for the police and obligation influence legal reasoning level?

• What is the connection between legal reasoning level and behavior?

Any significant explanation for law compliance needs to incorporate findings from the resiliency theory literature, including the impact of risk and protective factors known to be empirically linked to crime. Using selected risk factors, subsidiary research questions of the current effort are:

• To what degree do an increase in risk factors decrease or retard legal reasoning level?

• Does legal reasoning level mediate the negative influences of selected risk factors?

Chapter 2 will trace the theoretical development of legal socialization theory, providing more theoretical and empirical support

---

[4] The specific hypotheses and path model drawn from these general research questions are detailed in chapter five following a more detailed presentation of the theoretical and research literature.

for the link between legal reasoning level and important findings in the legitimacy literature. An overview of the logic and empirical literature framing resiliency theory will be offered in Chapter 3, highlighting further the connection between important findings in this area and legal socialization variables.

An overview of the theoretical basis for the larger Culture of Lawfulness project in Mexico from which the current data is drawn, and its origins in Sicily and Hong Kong is the focus of chapter four, providing practical applications of this study's themes. In order to contextualize the current research findings, this chapter also offers a more in-depth discussion of the legal context of Mexico, building on some of the themes presented in this chapter. Chapter 5 covers the research methodology and instrument validity. Chapter 6 will offer empirical support for the causal pathway suggested in the research questions. Finally, a discussion of the research, policy, and practice implications will be offered in the last chapter of the study.

Theoretical Perspectives-I: The Relationship between Legal Reasoning and a Legitimate Legal Context

Our Government is the potent, the omnipresent teacher. For good or ill, it teaches the whole people by example..... To declare that in the administration of the criminal law the end justifies the means – to declare that the Government may commit crimes in order to secure the conviction of a private criminal – would bring terrible retribution. (Justice Louis Brandeis, *Olmstead v. United States* (1928)

Introduction

Although the legal development theory (Levine and Tapp, 1977; Tapp and Kohlberg, 1977) at the core of the current study has its origins in cognitive development theory (Piaget, 1932; Kohlberg, 1969, 1984; 1986), and thus focuses principally on internal cognitive factors in explaining behavior, more recent findings and applications of the theory have emphasized the interaction with the socio-legal context in which learning takes place (Cohn and White;1997; Tapp and Kohlberg, 1977), even to the point of noting the connections to social learning theory (Akers, 1985; Bandura, 1969; Cohn and White, 1990).

The objective of this chapter will be to trace the origins of legal development theory, showing the important connections between its elements and key findings currently emerging from the legitimacy research (Tyler, 1990; Gibson, 1991; Cohn and White, 1997) that will frame the underlying theory of the core research questions and structural equation model briefly described in the previous chapter.

Beginning with Kohlberg (1969, 1976, 1984, 1986), and carrying through to the early formulation of legal development theory offered by Tapp and Levine (1974), role taking was offered as the principal means of interaction between the cognitive internal structures of the individual and the environment. The current chapter will draw on legitimacy theory to highlight the varying opportunities for role-taking available in different legal and class contexts, and thus expanding theoretical discussion on how legitimacy can impact upon legal reasoning level. The connections between legal context, legal reasoning and behavior will also be developed.

The Cognitive Developmental Paradigm

The origins of legal development theory are clearly found in the works of Jean Piaget (1932) and George Herbert Mead (1934) with both focusing on the social interactions that help define and predict behavior. This focus on social rather than physiological factors separated their work from much of the more behaviorally oriented theory in dominance at the time of their writing.

The concept of social interaction leading to the development of cognitive structures began with Mead (1934), who viewed the human personality as the product of the "acquisition of shared social meanings" (Ibid.). One begins the process of developing these meanings in early childhood, first through the learning of language, and later through exposure to the tremendous variety of social interactions characteristic of everyday life. Social interactions begin at their simplest, with the child focused solely on the immediate gratification of his or her needs. However, the child very quickly begins to learn to act and respond based upon an anticipation of the responses of others.

As the first agent the child interacts with in this manner is the parent, the child begins to learn and internalize the values of the parent through this process of "role taking". Over time, social interactions become more complex, and the child gains a social perspective that is based on a sense of "generalized others" rather than those strictly within his or her immediate framework. It is the opportunity for such social "role-taking" as a means of experiencing the environment, and its connection to the development of self, that is carried throughout both moral and legal development theories.

Piaget's (1932, 1983) early work on childhood learning and development began with an examination of how children learn to appreciate physical concepts such as space and causality; however, his work gradually extended into the realm of how they also acquire social and moral concepts. According to Piaget, humans mold themselves to the environment through a process of adaptation, in which the environment is shaped to their use. This reciprocal relationship between the individual and environment in which cognitive structures are developed to receive and organize information, is at the core of the cognitive developmental paradigm (Cohn and White, 1990). Most importantly, Piaget contributes the concept of developmental stages, in which an individual's capacity for organizing information becomes increasingly complex through this ongoing process of adaptation.

Piaget (1970/1983) offers three interactive processes by which this adaptation occurs. In the first stage (assimilation), the individual receives and assimilates information into existing cognitive structures. The information is then organized in such a way that the structures themselves can gradually evolve to reflect the individual's interaction with the environment based on the increasing complexity of information in a process of accommodation. A third process of equilibration ensures that that there is a continued balance between the often conflicting poles of individual cognitive structures and the variety of environmental stimuli.

As noted above, Piaget categorized this process of cognitive development according to three stages. In the earliest and most rudimentary preoperational stage, the individual's cognitive capacity is based entirely upon immediate experiences and the egocentric focus of the child. At this stage, language first begins to appear. Thinking becomes increasingly representational, and less dependent upon direct experiences as the child moves into the subsequent stages of concrete operations and formal operations. As Cohn and White (1990) note:

> A child's developing cognitive capacity...moves away from the concrete egocentrism of early interactions with the environment toward symbolic manipulation, but always within the framework of creating and re-creating the balance between the self and the environment (pg.31).

In other words, as the child becomes increasingly able to appreciate the different situational and experiential contexts of reality with increased cognitive capacity, he or she is able to recognize that there are different available perspectives of reality.

Although the previous work principally dealt with the learning of physical concepts and causality, Piaget (1932) would later translate this interactional framework to include the development of social perceptions and even moral reasoning. Two stages were offered to categorize moral development. Similar to some of the elements discussed above with respect to the preoperational stage, the first stage of *morality of constraint* is characterized by the egocentric interests of the child. Although he or she is able to curtail certain rule-breaking behavior in the anticipation of possible punishment, there is no higher-level moral thought; rules are complied with simply in a blind obedience to authority.

The *morality of cooperation* stage is said to occur once the individual is able to view the world from a variety of perspectives, including recognition of the need for equality across diverse groups and interests. The advancement between these two stages reflects an increased cognitive capacity, as well as a changing relationship with authority (Cohn and White, 1990; pg 32). Under a morality of constraint, the child is willing to accept even arbitrary and inflexible punishment from adults as being just (Ibid). Nonetheless, this stage must be successfully completed prior to progression to the morality of cooperation. However, through the processes of adaptation described earlier, the child begins to appreciate diverse perspectives, and is thus better equipped to look at authority and rules in a different light.

In accordance with Mead's emphasis on the need for adequate role-taking opportunities in order to facilitate mature cognitive development, Cohn and White (1990) state that "the extent to which children develop the morality of cooperation may be limited because adverse social conditions can deprive them of opportunities for reciprocal social interaction" (pg. 32).

The Origins of Moral Development Theory

Lawrence Kohlberg (1969, 1976, 1981, 1984, 1986) shared the cognitive orientation of both Mead (1932) and Piaget (1970/1983), including an emphasis on the processes of adaptation and learning through reciprocal interaction and equilibration.   However, unlike these theorists, Kohlberg's theory and research focus specifically on moral development, explaining how individuals reason about both general and legal moral dilemmas (Morash, 1978: 29).

According to Kohlberg, role-taking opportunities play a central role in the process of development; however, the individual him or herself can also play an important role in influencing the number of available opportunities by interacting with the environment. In this sense, cognition is "an active, connecting process, not a passive connecting of events through external association and repetition" (1969, pg.349).

Similar to Piaget, Kohlberg (1969, 1976, 1981, 1984) outlines three levels of moral development, comprising six stages representing different orientations towards the conventions and rules of society, and as such are referred to as preconventional, conventional and postconventional. Individuals progress through these stages as they increase in cognitive capacity, beginning in stage one with an egocentrism to both physical and social concepts.

It is important to note that Kohlberg saw these stages as representing an inherent logic and sequence to moral development, meaning that one cannot progress to a higher level without first having gone through the previous stages. Additionally, the cognitive capacity for distinguishing physical concepts comes prior to social concepts. As noted by Jones Brown (1996), "a child who has not reached the capacity for formal operational thought cannot take advantage of role-taking opportunities that are appropriate for developing conventional moral reasoning" (Jones Brown 1996: 35). Thus, one could argue that, "the experiences of some individuals and even the content or repressive character of some cultures can prevent or seriously inhibit moral development" (Cohn and White 1990: 34).

It is at the highest stages of cognitive capacity that an individual can be said to exhibit truly mature moral behavior. In the postconventional stage of reasoning, Kohlberg equates principles of justice to essentially the principles of role-taking discussed above. That is, in a specific situation, an individual's acts could be considered to be moral if they would still be the same regardless of the role he or she is playing within a given interaction and if, in advance, he or she did not know what role they would be playing. Kohlberg (1971: 213) notes that "morality viewed in this way is not that of the greatest good, nor is it that of an ideal spectator. Rather, it is a perspective shareable by all persons, each of whom is concerned about the consequences to him under conditions of justice". Under this concept of morality one would include the principles of justice, fairness, and reciprocity at the core of the procedural justice and legitimacy literature discussed below.

Thinking about Rules and Laws: From Punishment to Justice

As discussed in the previous chapter, the law can be used for coercive, immoral, and unjust purposes. However, in a rule of law society, the law can also be the mechanism for people to defend themselves *against* the interests of the powerful and unjust (Furnham and Stacey, 1991). Although many teenagers are unwilling or resistant to complying with laws or rules that they disagree with or that interfere with their activities, over time they become increasingly sensitive to issues involving unfairness, injustice, and human rights (Ibid).

Adelson, Green, and O'Neil (1969) found that younger children emphasized the restrictive, punitive aspects of laws and law enforcement. Between the ages of 13 and 15 youths in their study reported more abstract thinking about the law, understanding the community benefits of the law, and even of possible improper legal restriction of some of their liberties. By their late teens, youths in their sample began to "deal with the law in an even more abstract way, taking in the needs of the community, governmental practice and individuals, but they were wary of interference with their liberties" (Furnham and Stacey, pg, 156). These older respondents were best able to appreciate the changeability of ineffective or unjust laws through the processes of amendment or appeal.

This progression in the development of "values, attitudes, and behaviors toward the law" (Finckenauer, 1995) is best captured in the theory of legal development, first proposed by Tapp and Levine (1974), based primarily on the earlier work of Kohlberg. Although following Kohlberg's universal age-related sequence of stages, legal reasoning instead focuses more specifically on creating a "conceptual framework for interpreting, defining and making decisions about roles and rules, rights and responsibilities" (Tapp and Levine 1974: 22-23).

As with moral reasoning, the stages of legal reasoning do not themselves represent sets of specific beliefs about rules and laws. Instead, "each stage represents a qualitatively different organization of thought" (Tapp and Kohlberg 1977: 67), demonstrating ways of interpreting information as the individual interacts within a situational and environmental context. Although the possibility exists of legal reasoning being either accelerated or retarded as a result of the legal culture, such contextual variables cannot alter "the quality or order of these different modes of thinking" (Ibid.). Increasing stages of legal reasoning are said to reflect an increasing ability of the individual to resolve conflicts. The three stages of reasoning outlined by Kohlberg (preconventional, conventional, postconventional) are also used for legal reasoning, each with two stages.

The preconventional *rule-obeying* level is characterized by a deferential, fear of punishment orientation. Power is equated with justice, and as a needed means to maintain order. The first stage is called Physical Power (stage 1), and is typified by the strict punishment orientation noted above. Here there is an absolute deference to power and authority, regardless of circumstance. At the Instrumental Relativism stage (stage 2), the individual is guided by a hedonistic outlook, where satisfying personal needs and interests is paramount even though there begins to be some recognition of the need for equity and reciprocity in relationships (Tapp and Kohlberg, 1977). These preconventional stages are what is predominantly evidenced among children.

The conventional *rule-maintaining* level involves an active support of the established rules, norms, conventions, and arrangements of social order (Furnham and Stacey, 1991). Throughout this level there is very little tolerance for diversity or nonconformists. The conventional stages are the dominant form of reasoning for teenagers and adults. By the younger teenage years, stage 3 (interpersonal concordance) is prevalent, focusing on the need for approval and pleasing others. An emphasis on obeying rules and maintaining order is found in the Law and Order stage (stage 4). The functioning of the social system is the dominant concern here, with rules and laws binding an individual to society. At this stage, blind obedience is a possibility, although in some extreme circumstances such individuals may see a need to violate the rules or laws.

At the postconventional *rule-making* level, individuals readily recognize the distinction between laws, morals, and justice. Stage 5 reasoning (social contract) emphasizes a concern with the relationship between the individual and society, emphasizing the individual rights that are a pre-requisite to social arrangements and being governed. The final stage is referred to as the Universal Ethic stage because of its recognition that moral principles embodied in individual rights should always supersede other considerations, even at times, man made laws. Only a minority of adults reach postconventional stages of reasoning, and usually not before the college years. Later efforts, classifying moral reasoning into general schemas rather than strict stages, has found greater incidence of post-conventional thinking in the general young adult and adult populations (Rest, Bebeau & Thoma, 1999).

Furnham and Stacey (1991) stress that, consistent with Kohlberg's (1969) moral reasoning, each stage of legal reasoning is dependent upon experiencing the prior stages. However, they also note that this theory "assumes not only that the direction of moral development is towards internalized individual moral controls but also that the higher stages of morality move beyond dependence on culture and society to dependence on a selfless, rational, morally autonomous individual" (Furnham and Stacey 1991: 159). It is for this reason that the stages of reasoning are said to be correlated with law-abiding behavior where most criminal acts are concerned. However, it must also be said that at the highest postconventional stages acts of civil disobedience might still occur based on the individual's recognition of a division between justice and the law and a corresponding sense of "principled obligation" to violate (Tapp, 1987). The history of protest in the United States against such issues as the Jim Crow laws and abortion exemplify this distinction. In sum, there is a dynamic relationship between aspects of legal reasoning that have to be learned by the individual (with some influences from the rule-enforcing context), and those that require the awareness of others.

<u>Legal Reasoning Across Contexts: the Connection Between Legitimacy and Legal Development Level</u>

As noted throughout our discussion, legal development theory recognizes the important role that the environment can play in influencing the level of legal reasoning, even though the earlier work of Kohlberg (1969) and even Tapp and Levine (1974) principally observed the cognitive processes. Again, this interaction between the individual and environment is principally due to the "natural structuring tendencies of the organism" (Tapp and Kohlberg 1977: 66) first postulated as role-taking by Mead (1934) and other authors (Dewey, 1930; Allport, 1961; Kohlberg, 1969).

Tapp (1987) points to several important role-taking opportunities needed in the community to facilitate increased movement towards postconventional orientations in the population. Legal reasoning level is associated with developing "critical competence rather than conventional compliance" (Furnham and Stacy, pg.160). To achieve this state, Tapp recommends four community and school socialization techniques which provide the necessary role-taking opportunities to stimulate development.

The first approach simply involves transmitting knowledge of the law to youths; however, Tapp and Levine (1974) do stress that knowledge itself is a necessary, but not sufficient element to promote legal reasoning. Greater knowledge of the law leading to positive attitudes towards the law and consequently law-abiding behavior has been reported in some efforts (Law-Related Education, 1983; Zimmer and Huston, 1987), but completely unrelated in others (Rafky and Sealey, 1975; Jacobson and Palonsky, 1981; Markowitz, 1986). Despite increasing knowledge related to the law as children mature, attitudes toward the law and its enforcement are consistently found to get increasingly more negative as they reach adolescence (Portune, 1965; Markwood, 1975; Finckenauer, 1995; Jones Brown, 2000). "The students who know the most about the law are not necessarily those with the most favorable attitudes toward the law." (Palonsky and Jacobson, 1982: 27)

Part of these negative or inconclusive findings between knowledge of the law and attitudes might themselves be related to exposure to unfair or corrupt law enforcement practices as a youth begins to interact with or experience the force of the law first-hand.   Jones Brown (2000), in a study of 125 African American males and 25 white males, found that African Americans perceive the police as less legitimate than whites (Jones Brown, 2000: 95). As will be discussed below, such negative perceptions related to legitimacy might themselves prevent advancement in legal reasoning to postconventional levels. Moreover, these findings are possibly even more disturbing in that Jones Brown (2000) found that these negative attitudes towards law enforcement do not have to be the result of direct experiences with law enforcement. Rather, she noted "disturbing ripples (of negative attitudes) that emanate from the experiences of others" (Ibid., pg.99).

Tapp and Kohlberg (1977) note that the perceptions of law and justice incorporated into the cognitive structures of legal reasoning are very different in those who have had a sense of participation in the social order. In societies where corrupt practices are the norm, such needed opportunities for participation are non-existent, or even where they exist "on paper", citizens will develop a sense of helplessness in relation to the law and its enforcement. Such perceptions have been consistently noted with respect to African Americans, regardless of social class (Davis, 1974). These pervasive perceptions of inequality and injustice under the law have been used to explain how African American youths slowly come to de-legitimize the law over time (Davis, 1974, Jones Brown, 1996).

The fact that even middle-class African-Americans have been consistently found to view the social order as illegitimate (and in some case even more so than their lower class counterparts!) may be one explanation why research has failed to consistently demonstrate a link between legal reasoning level and class (Morash, 1978). Middle class African Americans may see the system as even more illegitimate given their higher exposure to the knowledge about the individual rights they are supposed to have under the constitution. However, exposure to such wide spread practices as racial profiling plays a significant role in their perceptions that equal protection does not exist under the law (Harris, 2002). As this recognition comes very early on in the lives of many African Americans, there may be a negative corresponding effect on their ability to progress to higher levels of legal reasoning. Although middle class African Americans are less likely to violate the law than lower class counterparts, this is likely due to the increased opportunities provided to them that on the one hand might lead to higher reasoning levels, and on the other brings about a greater attachment to conformity (Hirschi, 1969; Thornberry, 1994; Sampson and Laub, 1993; Jones Brown, 1996). It is possible, however, that the pathway between legitimacy, reasoning, and behavior may thus vary by class.

Based on these observations, Tapp encourages opportunities for youth to participate in decision-making related to rules, regulations, or laws within either a school or community setting. Such activities illustrate to students the complexities and imperfections of democratic participation, helping them to think in terms of the social responsibility and moral principles prevalent within a postconventional mode of thinking. Such activities also promote the needed critical thinking necessary for legal development.

Given the important influence of role models in guiding perceptions, Tapp stresses that the socialization context includes contact with adults that are exemplars of moral, fair, and just behavior. To the extent such adult examples can include the police, the better off the learning process will be. Interaction with just social agents is crucial according to Tapp and Kohlberg (1977) because it helps the youths to appreciate the inherent dilemmas and stressors of criminal justice, and law enforcement in particular. This is essential given that in even the most just society in which the rule of law predominates; there will always be contradictions and deviations. As society (government, law enforcement, judges, etc.) is governed by human agents, and human agents are themselves imperfect, there will never truly be a "pure" rule of law society (Godson, 1999). The key is to look at the principles of the rule of law as offering the best possible means to achieve a good quality of life, an outlook most consistent with level three thinking (NSIC, 2000).

Finally, exposing the youths to diverse perspectives and even conflicts with respect to rules and laws is also seen as integral to legal reasoning development (Tapp, 1987). This diversity can come in the form of "ideas, values, practices, and roles" (Furnham and Stacey, 1991:160) that promote cognitive development. Challenging youths with higher level thinking through such opportunities for conflict and resolution is the mechanism by which legal reasoning advancement is said to occur. As with the concept of cognitive dissonance, the youth is forced to reconcile the alternative mode of thinking with his or her own, and through the processes of assimilation and accommodation noted earlier (Mead, 1934) stage advancement is likely to occur.

Again, the stages must be progressed through sequentially, and youths cannot generally incorporate information higher than one level above their current stage of development. It has also been found that the greatest movement to higher stages occurs when the socializer him or herself is also one level above the learner (Blatt and Kohlberg, 1969; Turiel, 1997). The need for tailoring learning environments to the specific stages of development of the youths was also found by Turiel (1997), who noted that children are as likely to reject reasoning presented to them below their level "as to fail to assimilate reasoning and action too far above it" (Tapp and Kohlberg, 1977: 87).

Tapp and Kohlberg (1977) summarize the importance of a just, fair, and moral environment for adequate legal socialization in the following manner:

> The possibility of developing mature ethical-legal judgments is affected substantially by the credibility of the environment, whether it affords the opportunity for dialogue, sharing responsibility on decision-making. If such opportunities are negligible in these institutions, some individuals may be fixated at low levels of development while others ultimately

may seek conflict resolution across the barricades (rioters) and/or across the bars (delinquents) (Tapp and Kohlberg, 1977: 88-89).

From the perspective of the individual, legitimacy issues do not begin to become relevant until level two (Jones Brown, 1996). By legitimacy, this author subscribes to the definition offered by Friedrichs (1986) who states that it is "an affective belief in the obligatory quality of a social order" (Friedrichs, 1986:35). In other words, this conception of legitimacy refers to a legal order that is both deserving of and entitled to respect and compliance (Tyler, 1990; Jones Brown, 1996). As described above, the hedonistic, self-interested concerns of level one reasoning predominate over concerns of legitimacy. Power is authority and authority is justice. At this stage, the hedonistic calculus drives behavior, in which the likelihood of rewards is weighed against potential costs when deciding whether or not to engage in a particular rule-violating behavior. Thus, punishment is the reason for compliance rather than a respect for rules or differentiation between what is legal and moral (Tapp and Levine, 1977).

By level two, social conformity concerns dominate, with the individual following rules from within a law and order maintaining perspective. Although an unfair or corrupt government might be recognized as such, a level two individual might be likely to continue to obey authority because laws are needed to restrain the bad and hold off resulting chaos. The changeability of law begins to be recognized by stage four, in which laws that are not for the "good of all" because they permit unkindness, or are made by uncharitable persons, can be revised. Only extreme circumstances justify breaking laws or rules (Tapp and Levine, 1977). However, what can be said is that such a corrupt society would prevent individuals from recognizing the larger moral principles and fundamental individual rights perspective required for advancement to postconventional thinking. As noted previously, corrupt societies do not offer the needed role-taking opportunities for advancement in thoughts about rules and laws.

Empirical Findings of Legal Reasoning Level from a Cross-Cultural/
Cross-Context Perspective

As noted in the previous chapter, studies conducted in Turkey, Mexico, Taiwan, and the United States across both middle and lower classes (including illiterate villagers) found that there is universality to the stages of moral reasoning, despite obviously different legal contexts (Kohlberg, 1968, 1969; Kohlberg and Turiel, 1971). All three levels have been found to exist in different cultures. Preconventional (stage 1) characterized the thinking of the majority of children at age 10. Importantly, although youths in Mexico and Taiwan followed the same stages of thinking as those in the United States, by adolescence their rate of development was slower (Tapp and Kohlberg, 1977), suggesting the possible influence of differing contexts, particularly role taking opportunities. Although postconventional thinking could be readily found amongst American youths at the age of 16, the conventional morality stage continued to dominate thinking of Mexican and Taiwanese youths at the same age (Ibid).

Other studies comparing youths in Denmark, Greece, India, Italy, Japan, and the United States (Hess and Tapp, 1969; Minturn and Tapp, 1970) found that American preschoolers were predominantly preconventional in thinking, but progressed to a conventional orientation by middle school. By college, however, slightly over half could be classified within the postconventional framework of distinguishing between moral principles and the law (Tapp and Kohlberg, 1977). Although all studied cultures moved beyond the prescriptive focus of the preconventional mode of thinking, "the postconventional focus on the morality of the rule, which was strongly emergent by college in (American respondents), was not (found to be) a dominant cross-cultural justification for rule violation" (Ibid, pg. 83).

The possibility of cultural bias related to both the moral and legal reasoning constructs has often been raised over the last forty years. Authors such as Snarey (1985) argue that the higher stages of reasoning are focused on a justice orientation that will not be as prevalent in non-Western cultures that emphasize caring and reciprocity concerns in guiding social interactions. This is similar to Gilligan's (1982) argument that Kohlberg's moral reasoning scheme is inherently biased against women, given their larger emphasis on an "ethics of care" reasoning that is more characteristic of Kohlbergian stage three thought. This line of argument is dangerous in that it can lead to the evaluation of some cultures as being "morally inferior" in comparison to others (Simpson, 1974).

Kohlberg (1984) responded to such claims of cultural bias with the empirical evidence for the first five stages of reasoning across all studied cultures to date. However, as described above, the low prevalence of post-conventional thought in all cultures, but particularly non-Western ones, needs to be the subject of careful attention and research. It may be, as hypothesized by the current study, that societies with greater and more regular violations to the rule of law do not provide the requisite role-taking opportunities; future cross-cultural research will need to find innovative ways of separating out the effect of legal environment from general cultural factors. It should also be stressed that Kohlberg (1984) has also argued that higher stages of moral reasoning cannot be viewed literally as better than those at lower levels; higher stages can provide greater opportunity for solving a variety of conflicts, but this does not necessarily speak to judgments of greater moral worth.

The limited research in this area with respect to legal reasoning has actually produced findings contrary to expectations when comparing the legal reasoning of United States populations to other societies. Finckenauer (1995) sought to examine the influence of legal environments on legal socialization variables by comparing the attitudes, reasoning, and behavior of youths in the former Soviet Union, Russia, and the United States. This contrast is particularly interesting given the fact that the former USSR is an "example of one of the most totalitarian, coercive, and repressive legal cultures (of the twentieth century)" (Finckenauer, pg. 2). In contrast, the United States can be said to represent one of the more dominantly liberal contexts during the same period (Ibid.). Finally, a comparison between Soviet youths and their post-Glasnost Russian counterparts can examine the effects of a country transitioning towards democracy on legal socialization. Such comparisons across varying contexts are essential in that legal socialization is said to be "embedded within the law governed environment" (Cohn and White, 1990: 22), incorporating the "salient features of the legal environment" (Cohn and White, 1990: 189) such as fair enforcement of the rules, the legitimacy of rules, and the role of authority.

Contrary to expectations, Finckenauer (1995) did not find Soviet youths to be fixated in level one concerns of punishment and self-interest. In fact, Soviet youths reasoned at a slightly higher level (2.00) than American youths (1.92). Contemporary Russians also placed in the lower conventional level at 2.03 (Ibid). These findings match the cross-national findings of conventional level reasoning in youths between the ages of 10 and 14 (Tapp, 1970). As a frame of reference, Cohn and White's (1990) study of college students found reasoning levels in the range of 2.10 to 2.13.

Although Finckenauer's work failed to find a variance in legal reasoning across context, it may be that such differences are more noticeable as youths advance in age. Recall that the stage advancement of Mexican and Taiwanese youths started at the same pace as American youths, but progression towards postconventional levels slowed down (Tapp and Kohlberg, 1977). Other factors, such as the presence of risk factors were not examined for influence on reasoning level as will be undertaken in the current study. As Jones Brown (1996) found comparing black and white youths, Finckenauer's study (1995) revealed that Soviet and Russian youths were far more likely to be concerned with the reprehension of their families and peers than American youths. As this reflects a greater communitarian focus than the "doctrine of the individual" dominating United States legal discourse and possibly playing an influential role on legal reasoning level, future research should also examine this issue. Because such concerns with the acceptance of others is more characteristic of level two thinking, this too might be found to play a retarding affect on legal reasoning level should longitudinal or cross-age category research ever be undertaken again. More efforts need to be done to determine the degree to which differences in legal reasoning are influenced by context or cultural differences. This study hopes to be a continuing advancement in this area, laying the groundwork for later cross-cultural comparisons of its findings with the same instrument. Rest et al (1999), note that positive support for the cross-cultural applications of moral reasoning do exist (in that all three levels of reasoning have been found across diverse cultures), although there is a need for more empirical study.

The important influence of exposure to role-taking opportunities characteristic of differing legal contexts does exist, but work such as Finckenauer (1995) and Cohn and White (1990) demonstrate that it might be a complex pathway or relationship. Tapp (1987) found that exposure to and participation in the jury process increased the legal reasoning level of youths. Moreover, she concluded that the magnitude and direction of change in legal reasoning level depends directly on the role-taking opportunities available. A similar study by Morash (1978) failed to find such pre-post differences, but this can likely be explained by the fact that the intervention dosage only represented one day, hardly enough time to stimulate the necessary assimilation and accommodation processes offered by legal development theory as essential to stage advancement.

The study of university students living in varying conditions of rule enforcement (Cohn and White, 1990) briefly described in the previous chapter offers the most interesting support for the important role of rule-enforcing contexts on legal reasoning and ultimately behavior. To briefly recap, first year university students were randomly placed into one of three rule-enforcing environments: external authority, peer authority, and control. In the external authority, rules were strictly enforced by outside enforcers with no room for student participation or negotiation in the process. Zero tolerance policies of enforcement characterized the external authority situation. In stark contrast, the peer authority condition involved the students themselves participating in the process of creating and enforcing rules through participation on a residence council.

Importantly, Cohn and White (1990) found that the legal reasoning level of students in the external authority condition significantly decreased by the end of the school year. In addition, students in external authority dorms also had decreasing acceptance of the validity of enforcing various rules (enforcement status), as well as increased negativity to the rules themselves (normative status). In the peer authority condition, on the other hand, the legal reasoning level significantly increased in a positive direction. Additionally, residents in the peer authority condition were becoming more cohesive with respect to norms throughout the school year. This can likely be attributed to the fact that the peer authority residents were making judgments on the basis of the benefit to the larger community, an orientation characteristic of postconventional thinking. As a result, the normative status of both rules and their enforcement were seen as more acceptable under the participatory form of authority. This sense of community helps the students to become sensitized to the kinds of behavior that might be harmful to fellow residents (Cohn and White, 1990: 95), and creates a social responsibility that is a central ingredient in the needed value shift towards a culture of lawfulness (Godson, 1999), and is supported by the fact that there was less rule violation overall (though not significant) in the peer condition as will be discussed below.

Cohn and White (1990) note that the role-taking opportunities offered in the peer authority condition are what produce the key differences with respect to legal reasoning. In this condition, students were responsible for directly confronting the issues related to the fair enforcement of rules and holding people responsible for their actions (Cohn and White, 1990: 79).

In reviewing moral reasoning research across many cultures, Gielen and Markoulis (1994) claim that, "the main dividing line for the data is not between Western, Anglo-Saxon, English-speaking countries, but between industrialized Western or East Asian countries with demanding educational systems and Third World, less-industrialized countries with less-demanding educational systems" (pg. 85). However, as a word of caution, they also found that tests of moral reasoning in Egypt, Kuwait, and Sudan were contrary to the expectations of Kohlbergian stage theory. Authors such as Rest et al (1999) argue that moral reasoning is not a function of type of religion, but may be a question of orthodoxy versus non-orthodoxy. Postconventional thinking has been found across diverse faiths – the main area where religion can clash with higher stage thought is on the question of whether or not religious laws can be the subject of the interpretation of man based upon principles of human dignity and justice.

In sum, although it may be difficult to avoid making evaluative judgments related to a society's level of moral or legal reasoning, future cross-cultural research needs to try to separate out to the best degree possible the differing influences of role-taking opportunities in a society, as compared to general cultural beliefs. While research in this area overall is mixed, studies such as Cohn and White (1990) creatively highlight the importance of a legitimate legal context over general cultural concerns. Moreover, the larger body of empirical work has not tended to uniformly favor Western (particularly American) society to the degree that critics of Kohlberg, Tapp and Levine originally feared. Once again, the ties of the current study to a larger project across diverse cultures offer an exciting opportunity to examine some of these issues in greater depth.

Perceptions of Legitimacy: What are we looking for?

Utilizing public opinion polls, Gibson and Caldiera (1996) examine the relationship between the strength of democratic institutions in European countries (or legal culture), and the subsequent legal values of its citizenry such as the extent of legal alienation, the value placed on liberty, and the degree of support for the rule of law. In a related effort, Gibson, Duch, and Tedin (1992) study the political values of the Soviet Union, such as the degree of political tolerance, the value placed on liberty, the degree of support for competitive elections, rights consciousness, and degree of support for an independent media. Each of these values would be most likely to be found in the postconventional individual who views the world from a moral-rights perspective and the larger benefits to society.

The link between viability of legal authorities and the production of values supporting voluntary compliance with and respect for the law is found in a large body of empirical literature, particularly that of Tyler (1990). What this research demonstrates is that "people are more likely to accept legal decisions if they think they are *morally* (emphasis added) right and they are more likely to voluntarily accept decisions if they think that legal authorities are legitimate and ought to be obeyed" (Tyler, 2000: 914). Thus, Tyler's (1990) work argues that views about the morality and legitimacy of the law and its legal authorities such as the police and courts are crucial antecedents to securing voluntary compliance; the current study will examine morality within the context of legal reasoning level and legitimacy in terms of both belief in the fairness of the police and obligation to obey the law. This work will argue that perceptions of the fairness of legal authorities (legitimacy variable 1) can impact legal reasoning level either positively or negatively, which in turn creates legal values related to obligation to obey the law (legitimacy variable 2). Social responsibility is also hypothesized as being impacted by the connections between legal context and legal reasoning. Obligation and social responsibility thus serve as mediating attitudes between reasoning and behavior in line with the findings of Cohn and White (1990) discussed below.

The importance of legitimacy factors might also explain why deterrence factors have been found to have only a minor influence on behavior, as found in numerous empirical studies of both youth and adolescent populations (Nagin and Paternoster, 1991). It may be that deterrence plays a stronger role in those individuals reasoning from a preconventional level, but that this influence declines noticeably as one moves into conventional modes of organizing and contextualizing the legal culture surrounding him or her.

In making judgments about the effectiveness of legal authorities, the public is generally determining the overall fairness of both the creation of a rule, and its enforcement. The procedural justice model argues that people will be more likely to obey rules and laws that they feel have been created and enforced fairly. Tyler and Lind (1992) argue that with the relational model of justice, evaluations about procedural fairness emphasize the degree to which they have been treated with dignity and respect.

Importantly, much of the literature finds that the elements used to determine legitimacy do not significantly vary across cultures (Tyler, 2000). What is important is not whether or not we actually received the outcome we wanted (instrumental concerns), but rather the degree to which we perceive the decision-making mechanisms as fair. Additionally, the relational concerns of neutrality, trustworthiness, and willingness to respect group members have also been found to play a role in assessing fairness across cultures (Ibid.).

The instrumental concerns are most prominent when dealing with an "out-group" in society, making the need to enhance the identification of sub-groups with the larger society a paramount concern. Lind, Kray and Thompson (2001) argue that this can be best achieved by showing groups that they are included within the larger framework of society, and are thus valued and worthy of respect. Such identification might occur by civic education classes that demonstrate to children societal values and their role within the community, part of the legal knowledge elements outlined by Tapp (1987). The legitimate legal context will also play a significant role in influencing such judgments to the extent to which members of sub-groups see members of their own group being treated fairly and participating within the authority structures of the larger society. Such participation thus is part of the role-taking opportunities in society detailed in the above discussion.

<u>Examining the Pathway Between Legal Reasoning, Legitimacy and Behavior</u>

Palonsky and Jacobson (1982) concluded that being delinquent was only a moderate predictor of negative attitudes towards the law. However, the Law-Related Education Project (1983) found that attitudes toward the police were strongly correlated with self-reported delinquency. Similarly, positive affectations toward the police, courts, and the law have been found to be negatively related to some delinquency measures obtained through self-report (Brown, 1974).

Adding complexity to the relationship, some studies suggest that personal interactions with the police are not the only source of attitude formation towards the police. Jones Brown (2000) reported that African-American males in her study developed attitudes towards police through contact with their family and friends, or even through vicarious observations in the community rather than personal interactions. These findings may explain why, "modifying perceptions of police behavior may not necessarily improve actual interactions with the police" (Brandt and Markus, 2001). Attitudes towards police have been found to be embedded in feelings related to authority in general (Ibid).

Many studies have examined the vicarious effect of police misconduct on the development of negative attitudes towards the police (Baseheart and Cox, 1993; Kaminski and Jefferies, 1998; Jessilow and

Meyer, 2001). Although findings are mixed, the potential correlation between negative attitudes towards law enforcement and delinquency highlights the importance of improving police conduct in the community. The correlation between such attitudes and high neighborhood disorder and the presence of delinquent peers also needs to be examined.

In one of the most recent, large-scale empirical studies of legal socialization, Cohn and White (1990) conducted a quasi-experimental study within a campus residential setting. The researchers found no significant relationship between the level of legal reasoning and whether students were categorized as either rule violators or followers. They therefore concluded that legal reasoning is linked to law-abiding through "attitudinal mediators" (Cohn and White, pg.32).

The authors suggested that when individuals respected the "moral authority of the enforcer", they were also willing to "accept the legitimacy of its enforcement" (Finckenauer, pg.32). Cohn and White further suggested that where the rule enforcement was without "moral content", the level of legal reasoning of the enforced can actually be reduced (1990). Such findings complement Tyler's (1990) findings that perceptions of legitimacy were positively correlated with perceptions of obligation towards the rule and law structure.

Other studies, however, have found a direct correlation between delinquent status and level of legal reasoning. In his cross-cultural study of Russian and American youths, Finckenauer (1995) found that Russian delinquents did reason at a lower level than nondelinquents. To explain these results, Finckenauer states that "legal socialization offers a connection between a cognitive orientation that is self-centered (Level I), that views the law in terms of the risks of getting caught versus the personal benefits of law-breaking, and that does not view breaking the law as particularly harmful, as being stimulative of a greater propensity to break rules and laws" (pg. 162).

Tyler's (1990) Chicago study demonstrates the important pathway between perceptions of the legitimacy of laws and their enforcement and self-reported behavior. Those who see government and its agencies as deserving of respect are more willing to comply with its rules and laws. Moreover, where the public views the actions of law enforcement as generally fair, they are more willing to accept outcomes and comply with the decisions of authorities, regardless of whether or not it is individually beneficial for them (Ibid.). Thus, the conditions of unequal access to justice, brutality, and corruption briefly described above speak to more than just the morality of human rights. On a certain level, it may be that such factors themselves are helping to fuel much of the lawlessness they were created to protect against. In fact, perceptions of legitimacy may create a "cushion of support" that can help to mitigate against such conditions as poverty and unemployment that are known to play an incomplete role in decisions by individuals to engage in criminal activities (Ibid).

Although civic society has surfaced in many countries to protest the brutality and lack of available due process, these efforts often have been met with limited success due to larger public opinion or fear of the same lawlessness that law enforcement itself might be both directly or indirectly contributing to. "In many countries, preoccupation with a perceived rise in criminality and with the citizens' insecurity is fostering a dangerous tendency to justify police brutality or at least to consider it only an unfortunate fact of life" (Mendez, 1999). This trend in public opinion highlights even further population divide, in that it is more likely to be the sentiment of the middle and upper classes to whom the government and law enforcement have been able to convince that police abuses are only directed against the demonized, antisocial elements, usually drawn from the ranks of the poor (Chevigny, 1999).

<u>Summary</u>

In summary, although the legal development tradition borne out of cognitive developmental thought emphasizes the internal processes and structures that individuals use to organize, interpret, and interact with the environment, much of the theoretical and empirical literature in this area has demonstrated the important role that the environment can play in either facilitating or inhibiting legal reasoning development (Cohn and White, 1990; Finckenauer, 1995; Jones Brown, 1996; Cohn and White, 1997). Thus, societies that rely on corruption and coercion as means of ensuring compliance might be negatively influencing the degree of voluntary compliance, or lawfulness, in a country.

Advancement in legal reasoning requires access to adequate role-taking opportunities in society that can come in the form of participation in the democratic process, observation of fair and moral behavior on the part of legal authorities, and the opportunity to observe and respect the diversity of perspectives and experiences in a multi-cultural society.

Much of the recent work in the area of legitimacy (Tyler, 1990) has demonstrated the connection between compliance and perceptions of the fairness of procedures and processes. In contrast, empirical efforts describing the link between legal reasoning and behavior are much sparser and even conflicting. The most comprehensive study in this area by Cohn and White (1990) found that although the connection exists, it is mediated by attitudes related to the morality of the laws and their enforcement. Moreover, they also found that legal reasoning level was directly influenced by the legal context or "rule enforcing environment".

The current study will build on this work, highlighting the pathway between perceptions of the fairness of law enforcement (legitimate legal context), and legal reasoning. Obligation to obey the law and a willingness to act on this obligation (social responsibility) is of paramount importance in a society that does not wish to rely on coercion for compliance (Tyler, 2000). The current study will examine the degree to which the legitimacy variable of obligation does, in fact, serve as an attitudinal mediator between reasoning and behavior, much as normative and enforcement status was shown to in the work of Cohn and White (1990).

CHAPTER THREE

Theoretical Perspectives-II: Legal Reasoning as a Resiliency Factor

Introduction

A review of predictors of youth engagement in delinquent or criminal activity can quickly overwhelm a first reader trying to get a handle on the underlying causes or contexts of such behavior. Depending on the discipline of the researcher, one might find a host of empirical studies linking onset of criminal behavior to such diverse factors as pregnancy complications (Kandel and Mednick, 1991), attention deficit (Klinteberg, Anderson, Magnusson, Stattin, 1993), poor family management (Maguin, Hawkins, Catalano, Hill, Abbott, Herrenkohl, 1995), low bonding to school (Elliott, 1994), and delinquent peers (Farrington, 1989). Similarly, a review of the criminological literature, points to a host of central causal explanations for criminal activity ranging from blocked opportunities (Merton, 1968) and low self-control (Gottfredson and Hirschi, 1990) to learning through delinquent peers and community contexts (Akers, 1979).

The fact that both the empirical and theoretical literature can point to such a variety of criminogenic factors and explanations makes the prediction of crime very difficult. Even within the same contexts and same conditions, the majority of individuals do not end up involved in criminal or delinquent activity. Resiliency theory focuses on the factors that insulate individuals from crime despite criminogenic environments or characteristics. This chapter will provide a brief overview of some of the central components of resiliency theory, highlighting its plausible connections to the tenets of legal development theory outlined in the two previous chapters. The role of cognitive factors in current explanations of resiliency will be an important part of this discussion.

The Interaction Between Individual Characteristics and the Environment

Despite the large variety of predictor variables that have now been associated with crime, an increasing body of empirical work has indicated that the "characteristics of individuals interact with environmental influences and conditions to produce criminal behavior" (Reiss and Roth, 1993). Any meaningful theory of crime thus needs to be able to address key variables found within both the community and individual contexts.

Resiliency theory offers perhaps one of the most meaningful frameworks for organizing and understanding the often contradictory findings across the plethora of available predictor variables. As a result of its ability to synthesize interdisciplinary empirical findings, resiliency theory has also had a significant impact on practical programming on criminal justice policy and practice, including such major efforts as the Serious Habitual Offender Comprehensive Action Program (SHOCAP) developed in the 1990's to tackle chronic youth offenders. Successful juvenile gun violence reduction efforts have also drawn on the ease of application offered by resiliency theory (Sheppard, Grant, and Rowe, 1999; Sheppard, Kelley, and Grant, 2000).

The Office of Juvenile Justice and Delinquency Prevention (OJJDP) brought 22 leading researchers in the area of juvenile crime together for the creation of a Study Group on Serious and Violent Juvenile Offenders which released its findings in 1999. Following earlier work by Hawkins and Catalano (1992), the study group analyzed and synthesized current research on risk and protective factors (Loeber and Farrington, 2001). Predictor variables found to be associated with delinquent or criminal activity are termed risk factors (Hawkins and Catalano, 1992). Hawkins et al (2000), in their meta-analysis of the major long-term studies related to violence predictors converted the strength of correlations between risk factors and later violence into odds ratios, highlighting the practical applications of the resiliency theory literature. Odds ratios "express the degree of increased risk for violence associated with the presence of a risk factor in a population" (Ibid, pg. 2). For example, an odds ratio of 3 refers to a tripling of risk due to the presence of a particular risk factor.

The multitude of risk factors can be categorized across five domains: individual, family, school, peer-related, and community /neighborhood factors, as summarized in Table 1 (Hawkins et al, pg.2). This summary of risk factor domains is taken from Hawkins et al (2000). As noted above, there is a plethora of studies providing empirical support for the relationship between the risk factors and violence or other criminal activity that is beyond the scope of the current study context. Representing the connections across problem behaviors, these risk factors can also play a predictive role in behaviors such as substance abuse and teen pregnancy (Hawkins, Catalano, and Miller, 1992).

The logic of resiliency theory is that the larger the number of risk factors influencing an individual at any given moment, the greater is the likelihood of criminal activity or other problem behavior. Thus, programs seeking to reduce or prevent such activities will be most successful if they target multiple risk factors at the same time. Needs assessments clearly documenting the presence of all possible risk factors is an essential ingredient in selecting or tailoring programs to a problem that will have the greatest likelihood of success.

Table 1 Summary of Risk Factor Domains

DOMAINS	RISK FACTORS
Individual Factors	• Pregnancy and obesity complications; • Low resting heart rate; • Internalizing disorders; • Hyperactivity, concentration problems, restlessness, and risk taking; • Aggressiveness; • Early initiation of violent behavior; • Involvement in other forms of antisocial behavior; • Beliefs and attitudes favorable to deviant or antisocial behavior
Family Factors	• Parental criminality; • Child maltreatment; • Poor family management practices; • Low levels of parental involvement; • Parental attitudes favorable to substance use and violence; • Parent-child separation
School Factors	• Academic failure; • Low bonding to school; • Truancy and dropping out of school; • Frequent school transitions
Peer-related Factors	• Delinquent siblings • Delinquent peers • Gang membership
Community Factors	• Poverty • Community disorganization • Availability of drugs and firearms • Neighborhood adults involved in crime • Exposure to violence and racial prejudice

In contrast, protective factors refer to moderators of risk that increase the likelihood of positive, developmentally appropriate outcomes. Like risk factors, protective factors are also likely to occur together (Gore and Eckenrode, 1994). Rutter, Quinton & Hill (1990) notes that protective factors are often the antonyms of risk factors. Like risk factors, the number of risk factors occurring at a given moment will play an important role in the likelihood of criminal activity occurring. The more protective factors outweighing risk factors in a given context, the lesser is the likelihood of a youth becoming engaged in problem behavior.

The fact remains, however, that many youths resist the many risk factors they are faced with, and subsequent criminality, even while exposed to equal pressures across the five domains discussed above and living in a legal context ripe with corruption and brutality. Youths with very similar combinations of risk and protective factors occurring in their lives can have very different life courses. Researchers use the term resilience (Werner, 1994) to explain resistance to crime despite high-risk status. Earls (1994) describes the resilient youth as one with a higher IQ, easy temperament, attachment to and success at school, and at least one supportive adult. In addition to strong parenting fostering self-esteem, Werner (1984) highlights the presence of "skills and values that enabled (the child) to develop realistic educational and vocational goals" (pg.71). In adolescence, resilient youths are said to show superiority over their non-resilient comparisons in terms of an internal locus of control (Garmezy,1993; Luthar, 1991), academic behaviors (Lee, Winfield, and Wilson, 1991), and self-concept (Cohen, Wyman, Work, and Parker, 1990).

There has been significant debate as to whether or not resilience is "a state or a trait, whether successful coping in the face of adversity is domain specific, and what the psychic costs are for at-risk children who manage to grow into competent, confident, and caring adults" (Werner, pg. 115). Several studies have examined the degree to which resilience is multidimensional, using a number of variables simultaneously (Radke-Yarrow and Brown, 1993; Tiet; Bird & Davies, 1998).

Tiet and Huizinga (2002) found that when psychosocial functioning, self-esteem, academic performance, gang involvement, delinquent activities, and drug use were used as indicators of resilience and adaptation among a sample of inner city youth, two latent constructs emerged: adjustment and low level of antisocial behavior. However, they caution that due to the heterogeneity of the attributes being measured, creating a composite scale of these attributes would not be recommended.

Recent research has also shown how traditionally accepted protective factors such as self-esteem may not be as differentiating between criminals and non-criminals as once expected (Baumiester, 2001). Although some studies have shown that delinquent youths have a greater propensity for low self-esteem than their law-abiding counterparts (Wells and Rankin, 1983), others have shown the opposite; delinquent activities can actually enhance the self-esteem of participating youths (Kaplan, 1980; Rosenberg, Schooler & Schoenback, 1989; Tiet and Huizinga, 2002).

Taking Reasoning Seriously: re-examining the connections between legal development theory and resiliency

The resiliency factors identified thus far seem to suggest a cognitive superiority (Loesel and Biesner, 1990; Dubow and Luster, 1990) in resilient children that highlights a need to re-examine the cognitive developmental paradigm (Piaget, 1932; Kohlberg 1958, 1969, 1976, 1981, and 1984; Tapp and Levine, 1977) as potentially being a key ingredient in determining whether or not the imbalance of risk and protective factors ultimately leads to crime. For example, most longitudinal studies of resilient youths have found that both academic capabilities and intelligence, as measured by problem-solving and communication skills, are significantly associated with the ability to overcome high-risk situations (Block and Kremen, 1996; Freedman, 1988).

Werner (1994) notes that resilient youths "are better able to figure out effective strategies for coping with adversity, either through their own efforts or by actively reaching out to others to help" (Werner, pg.123). Although it is the least studied resiliency factor, the ways in which different styles of cognitive processing affect the consequences of high-risk situations has been noted as a research priority for the future (Rutter, 1987).

Recall that legal development theory focuses on "the individual's standards for making sociolegal judgments and for resolving conflicts, pressing claims, and settling disputes (Tapp and Levine, 1974: 4). The higher one progresses through the stages of legal reasoning, the greater the corresponding capacity to solve conflicts, critically think, and problem solve, making the possible linkages with current findings in resiliency theory quite clear.

The participation in experience-based activity involving conflict resolution, problem solving, participation in decision-making, and role taking influence compliance and independence in youths that extends beyond simply the uncritical law and order stage (Tapp and Kohlberg, 1977). Simply instilling obedience through "crime does not pay" approaches will only produce short-term gains because this fails to offer the needed learning modes of conflict resolution and participation discussed as facilitators for legal reasoning development in chapter two. The processes of assimilation and accommodation inherent to legal reasoning advancement require the gradual exposure to different points of view regarding right and wrong. With such opportunities, youths more readily internalize an obligation for law compliance, but are able to also balance this with a corresponding appreciation for their social responsibility and principles of justice (Ibid).

A possible connection to legitimacy theory is also evident in that the belief that teachers and authorities treat students fairly has been identified as a significant resiliency variable in some studies (McKnight and Loper, 2002). Moreover, the importance of future research emphasizing the connections between the resiliency and legal socialization literature is also hinted at by findings that resilient boys appear to come from households and schools where there is greater structure, rules and both parental and teacher supervision (Wallerstein and Kelly, 1980).

The key findings in evaluations of law related education programs reported on in chapter one also point to a connection between legal reasoning, problem solving, and resiliency. One evaluation of six law related education programs throughout the United States found that students were better able to solve problems and refrain from delinquency following participation in law-related education (LRE Project Exchange, 1982). Similarly, Chorak (1997) notes that the key ingredient of properly implemented law-related education programs is the promotion of social competence and cognitive problem-solving skills commonly cited in the resiliency literature.

It must also be stressed that the legal context can include both the formal and informal rule enforcing environments. Thus, the influences of family, peers, and community on legal reasoning are also important considerations in addition to the interactions with the formal legal authorities stressed throughout the first two chapters (Finckenauer, 1995). In this sense, the development of cognitive structures might include the social learning processes emphasized in the differential association (Akers et. al., 1979; Sutherland, 1955) and sub-cultural theories (Cloward and Ohlin, 1960). The fact that peer and family variables have been consistently identified as risk factors for crime and delinquency also make investigation of such linkages to legal development theory important.

Family management factors play an important first role in introducing children to rules and their enforcement. Much evidence supports the notion that parents of delinquent children punish more frequently, but inconsistently and ineffectively (Wilson and Hernstein, 1986). As a result, coercive and manipulative behavior can be reinforced at the expense of modeling prosocial behaviors. The emphasis on punishment could also theoretically play a significant role in locking a child in a preconventional orientation with respect to rules and laws, even as the child begins to be exposed to the larger community context. Fraser (1996) stresses that when children learn to respond to authority with aggression and manipulation, they will have difficulty interacting in the larger school and community environments. A harsh and rejecting parental approach to punishment has also been linked to delinquency (Patterson and Yoerger, 1993; Earls, 1994). Unfortunately, the pathways between such family factors and legal reasoning development have not been studied. Finckenauer (1995) and Jones Brown (1996) only reviewed family factors from the extent to which a child would feel guilty with respect to parental disapproval of conduct. Regrettably, these variables are beyond the scope of the current study as well, but deserving of future research.

High neighborhood rates of drug and gang activity, as well as other negative social influences are also consistently linked to delinquent or criminal activity (Sampson, Raudenbush, and Earls, 1997). Factors such as witnessing gang activity at school, or en route to school (Singer, Anglin, Song & Lunghofer, 1995; Embrey, Vazsonyi, Powell & Atha, 1996) are significant risk factors. Exposure to violence and criminal activity can retard legal reasoning development by overemphasizing the importance of power and manipulation in society, and thereby creating a sense of helplessness that is inconsistent with the critical thinking and appreciation of social responsibility required for advancement to postconventional thought. The link between poverty and reasoning may similarly be an understanding on the part of the youth that they are powerless to advance in society and thus the equality promised with individual rights and the rule of law is not a fair representation of reality. As a result, the value of peers and family will be deemed more important than that of the larger social context and morality (Finckenauer, 1995). Economic disadvantage is a consistent predictor of criminal behavior (Garrett, 1995). Although the current study will not be examining the influence of economic disadvantage on legal reasoning, it does incorporate measures of exposure to gangs and violence, as well as delinquent peer groups.

Low attachment to school has long been emphasized as a precursor to delinquency (Hirschi, 1969). The extent to which this risk factor is associated with legal reasoning level will also be examined. Although it is hypothesized that poor school attachment will play an inhibiting role on legal reasoning level, it is also equally possible that low legal reasoning will lead to low attachment to the rule structure of school environments.

As described above, a whole host of risk factors associated with individual characteristics have been identified in the literature, including biological and psychological influences. The current study will measure the association between self-esteem, locus of control, and legal reasoning level given their obvious theoretical connections to the legal context. Tyler (2000) notes that the perception that one cannot contribute to society, or that one's group is not valued in the larger social context can play a negative role on self-esteem. Thus, the degree to which one views the formal enforcement mechanisms as fair and deserving of respect could affect one's perception of self-worth. Similarly, an external locus of control in which one feels helpless in the context of social forces is both associated with delinquency (Werner, 1994), depression, and logically a preconventional or conventional orientation to the law.

Summary

The fact that the legal context includes both formal and informal mechanisms has been often noted in the legal socialization literature (Blasi, 1980; Cohn and White, 1990; Finckenauer, 1995; Jones Brown, 1996), but the pathways between informal social control mechanisms such as peers and family have not been adequately addressed empirically. Moreover, the potentially retarding effect on legal reasoning of exposure to lawlessness such as gang activity known to be associated with delinquency has never before been examined. The current study seeks to empirically integrate selected variables from the resiliency theory literature as part of the complex "micro and macro" context of legal socialization (Finckenauer, 1995). The ability of legal reasoning to "insulate" from empirically established risk factors will thus be examined (Morash, 1983).

In addition to the obvious theoretical connections between variables such as locus of control, delinquent peers and legal reasoning level, current research is consistently emphasizing the cognitive nature of the resiliency construct. Tapp and Levine (1977) have long noted the connection between legal reasoning and both problem solving and conflict resolution, providing additional support for the current study's re-conceptualization of the legal reasoning variable as a potential resiliency factor.

CHAPTER FOUR

Study Context

.....Our struggle showed that the law court is only one front in the campaign against violence and lawlessness. The other is culture. An image that occurred to me early in my own fight against the Mafia was of a cart with two wheels, one law enforcement and the other culture. If one wheel turned without the other, the cart would go in circles. If both turned together, the cart would go forward. So, at the same time as brave lawmen were dying in order to establish a rule of law, we were trying to rebuild our civic life (Orlando, pg.7). Leoluca Orlando, former Mayor of Palermo, Sicily.

Introduction

Up to this point, we have largely been discussing the theoretical connections that form the basis of the study, without a great deal of attention paid to the practical applications of this area of research. In fact, the inspirations for the integrated theoretical approach being tested come from the researcher's involvement in the evaluation and training of the Culture of Lawfulness project around the world as a consultant for the National Strategy Information Center (NSIC). Although this effort was briefly mentioned in chapter one, this chapter focuses on the origins of the culture of lawfulness model in areas as diverse as Hong Kong and Palermo, Sicily. At the same time as this chapter is meant to provide the reader with an orientation toward the overall study context, the case histories of Hong Kong and Palermo highlight the connections between the legal rule-enforcing context, legal reasoning, social responsibility and behavior that are the subject of this study's attention.

Moreover, the theoretical logic of the approaches to moral and legal education in combination with the efforts of civic society provides additional background for the study hypotheses that will be detailed and addressed in the last three chapters of this work. This chapter will also end by returning briefly to an overview of the legal context (i.e. nature and fairness of rule enforcement, legitimacy of rules, role of authority, and human rights generally) within Mexico in order to be better equipped for the interpretation of the study results in chapter six.

'Whacking' La Cosa Nostra through Moral Education: the role of Civic Society in Creating a Culture of Lawfulness in Sicilian Society

The Rule-Enforcing Context of Palermo, Sicily:

Throughout the 1980s and early 1990s in Palermo, there were more victims of organized crime violence than victims of terror in such torn world locations as Palestine or Belfast, numbering into the thousands (Orlando, 2001); included amongst these victims were "the general in charge of security forces, the chief of detectives, the chief of police, and two of the most famous magistrates in Europe"(Orlando, pg.1). Spurred on by a desire to control narcotics traffic between an organized crime network headed by Gaetano Badalamenti and a growing number of younger bosses, known as the Corleonisi[5], the resulting violence was coined the "Mafia war", and "involved a level of aggression that (even) many Mafiosi consider(ed) a betrayal of Mafia, although violence has always been intrinsic to this institution" (Schneider, pg.2).

Existing as an institution in Sicily since the nineteenth century, the Mafia had come to permeate all aspects of civil society, including social, political, and cultural life (Schneider, 1998). The established networks eventually began to take on the functions of government,

---

[5] Mafia families have been historically territorial, taking on the name of the place of their origin, in this case, the rural town of Corleone.

collecting taxes, creating a complex organizational hierarchy, and developing its own groups of "enforcers" to ensure compliance with its demands (Orlando, 2001). It was considered the right of the Mafia families to extort a tax (known as a *pizzo*) on all business activities within its territory, in addition to ensuring that employers hire selected Mafia dependents if desired. The Mafia also served the role as mediator of conflicts, even returning stolen goods (for a fee) on occasion (Schneider, 1998).

Leoluca Orlando (2001), the former mayor of Palermo, notes that a major factor in the Mafia's ability to dominate Sicilian life in such a complete way was the result of its ability to translate a mystique to the general populace. Its members were portrayed as Men of Honor that were integral to the smooth functioning of society (pg.11). This mythology surrounding their actions allowed them to see their jobs as a "call to duty" in much the same way as one might think of becoming a police officer or firefighter. As a subculture, Mafia values were translated through a rule of secrecy embodied in the word omerta, "silence before the law" (Schneider, pg.1). So strong was this force that it was unheard of to openly discuss the existence of the Mafia. In fact, it was not until 1982, after over a hundred years of Mafia domination, that the Catholic hierarchy began to speak out against the "evil institution" on the island (NSIC, 2000).

Because political and economic life had adjusted over many years to the presence of the Mafia as part of the regular social order, law enforcement would be faced with a dual challenge when it finally decided to assert itself against this force (Orlando, 2001). In addition to traditional law enforcement investigative and prosecutorial approaches to combating organized crime, it would have to first redefine the reality of the mafia as "criminal" (Ibid, pg.11).

As a result of corruption and Mafia domination, Palermo had become a wasteland of sorts, with deteriorating public services, crumbling monuments, overcrowded schools, and high crime. However, walking the streets of Palermo just ten years later paints an entirely different picture:

> The sidewalks are packed – every day and every night. Underscoring the upbeat tempo, music blares from

loudspeakers atop utility poles. Shoppers patronize storefronts that line the streets of a city that has never experienced such prosperity – even though the unemployment rate is 29 percent (Wood, pg.1).

Further testament to a sea change in such a short time that has now been characterized as the "Sicilian Renaissance" (Godson, 2000), is the fact that the municipal debt rating service, Moody's, upgraded Palermo's bond rating to Triple A, noting the tremendous political, legal, and economic reforms that have helped to restore investor faith in its integrity and economic potential for development (Wood, 2001).

The Pendulum of anti-Mafia movements:

As a result of the extreme violent toll on Palermo society following the Mafia war in the early 1980's, 460 mafiosi were prosecuted in Palermo's "maxi-trial" (Orlando, 2001; NSIC, 2000; Schneider, 1998), greatly damaging major Mafia family networks throughout Palermo and some parts of southwestern Sicily. The use of pentiti, or Mafia informants, proved essential in achieving the conviction of the majority of those indicted; and, importantly, these convictions would hold on appeal.

However, this intensive law enforcement crackdown was also supported by a growing anti-Mafia social movement based in Palermo that would include a series of conferences, demonstrations, and commemorative events designed to "create a new collective identity that overpowers the negative, centuries-old Sicilian stereotypes of criminality and violence" (Wood, pg.1). Such efforts included the vigilance of Mayor Orlando and the anti-Mafia party he founded, *La Rete*; a network of social centers operating in the poor neighborhoods of Sicily's major cities; and, the "Committee of the Sheets" building on the actions of a group of sisters and daughters that hung slogan-painted sheets and placards from the balconies of their neighboring apartments on the evening of the assassination of the prominent anti-Mafia prosecutor, Giovanni Falcone (Orlando, 2001; NSIC, 2001; Schneider, 1998).

Schneider (1998) tracks the multi-faceted nature of the anti-Mafia movement, describing it as a "growing social force that widens and branches in response to violent events, then contracts and fragments under the returned weight of 'normalcy'" (Schneider, pg. 4). As described briefly above, the maxi-trial and subsequent societal backlash against the Mafia in the mid-1980s is seen as a time of the "Palermo Spring", in which Orlando is serving his first term as mayor, and the momentum for political and social change seems ever-present. Despite this, both Orlando and Schneider describe the late 1980s as a period of "retreat and backlash" (Schneider, pg.5), in which the Mafia fought to regain its foothold on Palermo society. At the same time, efforts to investigate and combat organized crime, such as the Antimafia Pool began to be dismantled (Orlando, pg. 133), thereby crippling the fight against the mafia.

It was with the 1992 deaths of two leading anti-mafia fighters, Giovanni Falcone and Paolo Borsellino, that the public would be changed in a way such as had never before witnessed, leading to the birth of the Committee of the Sheets and other efforts described above. Orlando relates:

Always before, Sicily had been caught in a pendular history – long periods of equilibrium broken by episodes of violence, followed by a new commitment on the part of the government to control the Mafia, which always eventually failed. But something changed with the deaths of Falcone and Borsellino. This time it seemed possible that the Mafia pendulum would not swing back again (Orlando, pg.183).

The deaths of Falcone and Borsellino thus served as a catalyst for many segments of Palerman society to take action against the organized crime and corruption that had paralyzed them for decades. Such efforts of protest in the face of threat and injustice reflect larger principals comparable to postconventional thinking. It can be argued that additional stimuli for this movement in civic society lay in the recognition that serious efforts were being made to reform government generally, and law enforcement specifically, helping to move many Sicilians away from the learned helplessness and denial that had previously characterized their existence. Over time this effort to rebuild neighborhoods and the city as a whole would require the combined efforts from all sectors of society, including the business community, faith-based community, law enforcement, government agencies, the media, and the schools.

Educating for a Culture of Lawfulness:

In addition to the rising public sentiment against lawlessness and organized crime, the media began to expose and condemn the Mafia and its political and law enforcement collaborators, further contributing to an environment in which it was now possible for citizens to realize that they had the capacity to reverse "even well-entrenched and corrupt criminal behavior" (NSIC, pg.7). Local newspapers such as the *Giornale* which had formerly refused to acknowledge the existence of the mafia suddenly began to run articles supportive of change.

This provided politicians with further fuel to seek legislative change to eliminate many years of corrupt practices. For example, the city established rules that ensured all employees owed their jobs to their qualifications rather than connections to organized crime figures (Orlando, 2001). Sicilian law recently changed the age-old method of having the regional parliament appoint the governor, a system that the mafia was able to control to their interests, providing for the direct election of the position for the first time (Wood, 2001). Other laws were changed to make associating with the Mafia a crime and providing governmental agencies the authority to confiscate the property of organized crime families, similar to the RICO statutes later used in the United States. Collectively, people began to recognize the positive role they can play in government and community change initiatives.

Perhaps surprising to many observers is the integral role that teachers in the public schools played in the overall change efforts. According to a Palermo councilman and teacher,

> The only way to fight against Mafia arrogance, the only way to fight against violence, is to repeat the concept that freedom comes with dignity and justice. Education is the most

powerful tool we have in this fight (DiPalermo as cited in Wood, pg. 5).

As noted above, the schools were allowed to deteriorate along with the rest of the city as a result of corrupt practices, such as the severe under-utilization or misappropriation of resources available for the construction of new schools (Schneider, pg.5), creating inadequate conditions for learning. School conditions consequently became a central focus of the Orlando reform effort in 1995.

Although legislation was passed as early as 1980 providing public funding for anti-Mafia projects and "education for legality" in elementary, middle, and high schools (Ibid.), by 1988-89 only 12.5% of eligible schools had applied for these funds. At its peak following the maxi-trial, the numbers quickly fell off as time passed, providing further evidence for Schneider's (1988) observation of a pattern of "normalcy and backlash" in the anti-Mafia movement. Some teachers challenged the need to have the Mafia as a curriculum or extra-curricular activities topic.

Real reform efforts were concentrated in the middle schools, reflecting the "greater openness of schools.....whose constituents are neither little children in need of a lot of guidance, nor young men and women in the late stages of preparation for specialized educational or career choices" (Schneider, pg.9). Alongside the growing environment for reform following the 1992 murders, the middle schools were reinvented, according to Schneider (1988), with the "infusion of younger teachers and administrators sympathetic to educational democratization" (pg.10).

Arguably the most significant development with the emerging legality education movement in the schools was the concentration of strong efforts in many schools in the highest risk, most Mafia influenced locations. In addition to the many challenges offering such programming in these areas, teachers had to deal with students from Mafia backgrounds who felt singled out or ostracized by the curriculum (Schneider, pg.10). The similar efforts in Mexico described briefly in this chapter also uncovered this difficulty, highlighting the need for strong teacher support and solidarity for negotiating the difficult issues that are sure to arise when addressing these issues head on (Schneider, 1998).

The effort in the public schools seeks to teach students about good citizenship, and why adhering to a culture of lawfulness ultimately makes for greater prosperity, even though it may involve delayed gratification (Woods, 2001). To accomplish this goal, and instill a requisite pride in Palermo's ethnic and architectural heritage, the city offered the "adopt a monument" program in which school children learned the history of city landmarks and oversaw their restoration from deteriorated states (Wood, 2001; NSIC, 2000). Tours of the revitalized landmarks are then given to area residents. It can be hypothesized that the government's attempts to revitalize the city and reduce disorder served to begin the process of restoring civic trust in government and the possibility of the rule of law in Sicilian society.

A concentration on citizenship also involves traditional law-related education elements such as learning what their civil rights are, and the importance of exercising them, such as the right to vote (Schneider, 1998). The programming also confronts the Mafia subcultural values of vindicating wrongs and harboring grudges by emphasizing conflict resolution skills. However, most importantly, students are taught to denounce violence and crime, and report wrongs witnessed to authorities in stark contrast to the omerta philosophy passed on for generations.

Schneider (1998) correctly notes the need for a more interactive methodology in addressing these concepts, providing the example of student engagement in rule-setting with the principal in one school. This is reminiscent of the approaches advocated by Tapp (1970) to encourage the advancement of legal reasoning in youths. Additionally, students learn the history of organized crime and its consequences on Sicilian society, in efforts to "de-mystify" the Mafia mythology for the youths (Ibid.). In addition to the adopt a monument program, other events include exhibitions protesting violence and narcotics, and a day designated in honor of Falcone and Borsellino and their important work on the maxi-trial and overall anti-mafia legislative reform (Wood, 2001).

A Silver Bullet? The results of cultural renewal in Sicily:

Introducing himself to a United Nations convention on transnational crime, Leoluca Orlando stated, "The Mafia always tried to be the real face of Sicily, but they are not the real face of Sicily – they are the real enemy of Sicily. The Mafia is still present, still dangerous, still living, but the Mafia no longer controls the minds of the population" (as cited in Wood, pg.2). Although no one can expect to completely eradicate such problems in a short period of time, it is clear that Palermo has made significant political, economic, and legal strides towards ridding itself of its mafia-dominated legacy. Networks still exist; particularly in rural Sicilian towns outside of Palermo, but their strangle-hold on this increasingly prosperous city appear to have lifted significantly. It is also clear that the school-based component to a system-wide anti-mafia movement played a very important role.

Schneider (1998) carefully argues the virtues of the anti-mafia movement in Palermo schools, but through interviews with parents and students, also presents the readers with some cautionary words. First, in some neighborhoods as many as 40% of youths do not attend school or drop-out before the legal age of 14. While these are the same kids at the greatest risk for involvement in organized crime or delinquency, as noted above, they will not be exposed to much of the anti-mafia movement's school-based efforts.

Additionally, many working class parents told her that the mafia provided them with work, whatever its source may have been. Without this resource, there has been a rise in unemployment that has made their lives miserable. In fact, some interviewees claimed that there was actually an increase in street-level delinquency due to the lack of available jobs. One of the principals claimed that the "external world disqualifies the message of the school" (As quoted in Schneider, pg.20). Each of these issues also surfaced during focus groups with the teachers and students in Mexico participating in the larger current study, and will be addressed in later chapters in relation to the data analysis of legal reasoning, legitimacy, and behavioral variables. It supports the arguments of the previous chapters that efforts to combat crime and corruption cannot be the responsibility of only one sector of society, whether it is the police, schools, church, etc. Efforts only drawing upon one sector, however well intentioned and planned, will ultimately fail without larger support and collaboration. This is similar to the findings in the risk factor literature outlined in the previous chapter; there is a need to work across multiple risk factor domains in order to have long-term, sustainable reductions in crime or other related problem behaviors.

Despite these critiques, the obvious successes in Palermo warrant future replication and study across other contexts, as the current project in Mexico (and expanding around the world) intends to do. Attention to the specific components of such programming leading to behavioral change and resilience in participating youths will be the foundation for the current project described in the following chapters. The tremendous step made by Palermo towards establishing a lawful society is embodied in a final quote by Wood (2001):

> The Corleonese Mafia once was reputed to be the strongest Sicilian crime clan, but today its old-line leaders are imprisoned or fugitives from justice, and those who have taken their place keep well out of the public view. No more is the town square empty, citizens intimidated by decades of lawlessness, officials said as they detailed how the transformation, begun 30 years ago, has taken hold (Wood, pg.5).

A Three-Pronged Approach to Civic Reform: Hong Kong's ICAC Model

Given the many contextual factors that contribute both to underlying problems and/or the success of strategies to combat them, it is important to examine the applicability of efforts across differing contexts. What components have been similarly effective? What areas need to be modified to better suit the particular dynamics of a given community or even country? Moreover, will what has worked elsewhere also work here? Why or why not? These questions are particularly salient as technical assistance or training packages are translated and delivered internationally.

Despite their very different cultures and contexts, Hong Kong and Palermo, Sicily have a lot in common when it comes to innovative, systemic approaches to combating corruption and crime through civic reform and law enforcement. In the early 1970s, several very well-publicized scandals revealed that both the government and private sectors had rampant corruption, including the police force itself. In response to these issues, the Independent Commission Against Corruption (ICAC) was established in 1974, quickly rising to become one of the largest anticorruption forces in the world with a staff of over 1,200 (Lo, 1999).

The ICAC strategy involves three departments with specific functions, including a central administrative unit coordinating activities: the Operations Department, the Corruption Prevention Department, and the Community Relations Department. Transparency International Global Corruption Report (October, 2001) describes ICAC as a "model anti-corruption agency". Most importantly for our purposes, however, is the fact that the public support rate for the ICAC fluctuates at around 99%, providing evidence that the "culture of intolerance of corruption has firmly taken route in Hong Kong" (Ibid). Civic society is now less prepared to blindly accept the practices of the corporate and government sectors, and more likely to report violations of fairness and justice in society.

ICAC will investigate potential corruption cases in both the private and public sectors, enforcing a zero-tolerance approach intended to "level the playing field" for business in Hong Kong (Ibid). To do this, technical assistance is also provided to help government and public agencies to rid themselves of opportunities for corruption, as well as to help private companies to develop strong mechanisms for internal accountability.

Operations Department

The Operations Department is the largest, and with its responsibility of receiving and investigating all complaints of corruption, it also attracts the most intense public and media interest in major cases (Chan, 1998). Like major police departments in the United States, the ICAC can receive complaints from numerous sources, including a 24-hour hot-line reporting center (Ibid).

Corruption Prevention Department

This department is responsible for reviewing the practices and policies of both government and private agencies in order to promote "corruption-resistant management and administration systems" (Chan, pg.367). The department seeks to offer corruption prevention to public and private entities by making their activities more transparent to employees and the public, as well as creating sound, consistent formal policies and procedures.

Community Relations Department: anti-corruption education

Most relevant for our discussion, are the efforts of the Community Relations Department, as it is responsible for the public education and publicity functions of the Commission. The large-scale anti-corruption attitudes of the citizenry did not develop overnight, involving extensive media and community-based programming by the ICAC over the last almost thirty years. Through this department, the ICAC is readily accessible to the community through regional offices that provide the opportunity for direct community input.

Similar to the efforts in Palermo detailed above, ICAC developed a series of moral education modules designed to teach youths the requisite knowledge and values required to become a good citizen, including developing proper attitudes towards the importance of material goods and overall fair play (Lo, 1998). Targeting youths between the ages of 16 and 18, the Community Relations Department works with the school system and professional teachers to offer the moral education lessons through a variety of mediums. In addition to regular lesson plans, ICAC officers offer educational conferences in moral education, and maintain close contact with teachers and educational organizations in order to "gauge current trends and development in moral education" (Lo, pg. 2). On-going resources are provided by the ICAC for the development of teacher support materials. Other program packages include formats for assemblies and teacher periods, with follow-up discussion format facilitator guides available for both teachers and parents.

Although the school-based efforts began with a ten-lesson program taught by ICAC officers in selected schools, it later evolved to a "whole-school approach" with teachers being responsible for teaching the social ethics components within the formal and informal curricula, and the ICAC officers remaining responsible for the legal aspects of anticorruption education (Lo, 1998). The curriculum was designed to follow a "three-stage progression from understanding, to judgment to application" (Ibid, pg.3). Table-2 (Source: Lo, 199 (pg.3-4)) illustrates how moral education has been integrated across the curriculum.

Table 2 A Cross-curriculum Approach to Moral Education

Academic Subjects	Topics	Moral Education Objectives
Social Studies	Social problems – crime	Encourage pupils to help fight crime
Health Education	Mental health	Help pupils to understand their strengths, weaknesses, and learn to accept successes and failures
Mathematics	Measurement of angles	Help pupils understand the concept of citizenship
English	Making simple statements	Help pupils accept duty and responsibility, fulfill obligations, and exercise rights
Music	Song composition	Help pupils understand the importance of responsible behavior in social interaction
Physical Education	Ball game	Help pupils understand the importance of cooperation and rule-abiding

The overall philosophy of the ICAC moral education packages is that "corruption is a social evil stemming from weaknesses in personal morality" (Lo, pg.5). A connection to the development of legal reasoning is explicitly noted by the ICAC, with the idea that enhanced judgment will be practiced by the youths as they encounter daily issues in their interactions with peer, family, school, and social contexts (Ibid.). Lo (1998) summarizes the following core social values targeted across program packages:

- Balanced view of wealth and material possessions
- Regard for truth and honesty
- Regard for justice and fairness
- Regard for the rights and welfare of others
- Awareness of one's rights
- Sense of responsibility
- Respect for the rule of law
- Concern for the welfare of the community

The compatibility between these components and the theoretical underpinnings of this study need no explanation. Like the Palermo educational effort, ICAC provides less emphasis on traditional classroom methods, and more on interaction and reflection through role-playing and problem-solving approaches. This is important, given the necessary role of cognitive dissonance and active student participation in legal reasoning advancement discussed in chapters two and three. Additionally, the program packages continue to be modified in response to changing social and legal contexts. For example, modifications were made to materials after the 1984 decision to return Hong Kong to China and the Tiananmen Square massacre (Lo, 1999).

As found in Palermo (and Mexico, as will be described below), ICAC stresses that the successful implementation of the curricula in the schools invariably relies upon the attitude and cooperation of the school administration and other teachers (Lo, 1998). In some cases, the program fell under the weight of Hong Kong's intense examination pressure and the need to cover regular curricula completely.

Replicating Best Practices: Fostering a Culture of Lawfulness along the U.S/Mexico Border

As discussed earlier, it was based upon these successes that the Ministry of Education of Baja California, Mexico, and the San Diego County Office of Education (Sweetwater District), and NSIC brought together teachers and education specialists from both sides of the border in 1998 to develop and implement a pilot curriculum to increase children's knowledge of crime and corruption, as well as strengthen their support for the rule of law and a culture of lawfulness. To briefly recap, the originally developed curriculum was piloted in 1999 in Tijuana schools and Sweetwater District, San Diego reaching more than 814 students in its first year (Godson and Kenney, 2000). Building on program elements shown to be successful in Hong Kong and Palermo, this original curriculum was a 36-lesson course categorized into three related parts:

- Values, Self-Esteem, and a Culture of Lawfulness;
- Organized Crime and Corruption; and,
- Furthering the Rule of Law, Resistance Techniques, and What Students Can Do (NSIC, 1999; Godson and Kenney, pg.4)

A rigorous quasi-experimental evaluation design was conducted to measure the impacts of the curriculum on the participating students, and to inform subsequent program modifications. Students in both participating and control schools were administered an instrument in two waves, including five scales from the *Effective School Battery* (Gottfredson, 1991). The first administration took place prior to beginning the program in August and September, 1999; the second took place in December 1999 at the conclusion of the course (Godson and Kenney, 2000).

Pre/post measures of student changes in peer associations, belief in rules, interpersonal skills, and positive self-concept were collected as per the logic of the overall project goals. In addition, 39 subject matter questions were included to document changes in knowledge following participation in the course. Also significant, the evaluation instrument had a seven-item scale used in a large-scale cross-cultural effort designed to measure changes in legal reasoning (Finckenauer, 1995). Based upon the open-ended instrument originally used by Tapp and

Levine (1974), this scale classifies respondent legal reasoning into three hypothesized levels: preconventional, conventional, and postconventional.

The revised 60 lesson Culture of Lawfulness curriculum builds on the successes and lessons learned during the piloting of the program in schools throughout Baja California, Mexico and Sweetwater District, California in 1999 (see Godson and Kenney, 2000). The new Culture of Lawfulness program has four interconnected components as described in Table-3. In its revised incarnation, the program's curriculum retained the pilot version's underlying theoretical framework and focus, while at the same time increasing from 36 to 60 lessons.

Additional lessons clarified the distinctions between key concepts such as the rule of law and culture of lawfulness. Moreover, the mechanics of problem-solving were refocused in the course's final section to engage students in the practice and comprehension of each of its four stages (identification, analysis, response, and evaluation).

The demonstrated ability of the program to improve student's knowledge related to crime and corruption, as well as influence some attitudinal changes has led to the expansion of its piloting across new cultures and contexts. Beginning with just 8 schools in Tijuana during the piloting, the 2000-2001 school year included 209 classrooms in four municipalities (Ensenada, Tecate, Mexicali, and Tijuana). During the evaluation period, a fifth municipality (Rosarito) was added, but too late to be included in the current study.

As noted above, since this time the Culture of Lawfulness program has expanded to other states throughout Mexico (and since around the world), reaching thousands of secundaria students each year.

The findings of the second large-scale evaluation, from which the current data is drawn, indicate continued support. The next section will present those findings that have relevance to the hypotheses of this study.

Table 3 Structure and Theoretical Progression of the Culture of Lawfulness Curriculum

SECTION	DESCRIPTION	EXPECTED OUTCOMES
Values and Lawfulness	The curriculum begins with the recognition that increased knowledge about crime and corruption, its consequences on society, as well as the reasons for rules and laws will foster both an appreciation and moral support for a culture of lawfulness (Finckenauer, 1998). The challenges in conveying this message in contexts where crime, corruption, and poverty are pervasive, and the presence of gangs and narco-trafficking are everyday realities, requires first developing an appreciation in students for who they are, and the impact of their decisions on their lives. Section One thus focuses on the students' ability to impact their own lives. Beginning with the process of self-reflection, section one of the course challenges students to examine both their values and associations.	• An appreciation of the importance students can play in affecting their own lives as well as the community around them (i.e. decreased fatalism, increased internal locus of control) • A stronger sense of one's self and values is expected to lead to self-assurance and increased self-esteem, providing a basis for making sounder decisions in one's life.
Culture and Lawfulness	Section II builds on this foundation, helping students to recognize the differences between rule of law and a culture of lawfulness, as well as the importance of each in achieving a sound quality of life. The end of the section links students back to the importance of values and choices related to	• An appreciation for the importance of a culture of lawfulness and their role in contributing to it • An increase in students' sense

SECTION	DESCRIPTION	EXPECTED OUTCOMES
	moral dilemmas when laws and one's own sense of morality might conflict. An important theme of this section is not only a recognition of the importance of a culture of lawfulness, but also getting students to appreciate their own social role in contributing to it through their own participation within the community and the democratic process in general.	of social responsibility. • An orientation favorable to rules and laws
Crime and Corruption	Following the third section of the course, students should be able to understand the nature of organized crime and corruption, as well as its impact on a culture of lawfulness. By understanding the structure and nature of organized crime, it is hoped that students are able to recognize its ultimate impact on their communities. In addition to not tolerating such activities and their influence, students learn the potential contributing role they can play through public demand and tolerance of such activities. This section sets students up to understand the need for the "two wheels of the cart" utilized in Palermo, Sicily to combat the influences of the Mafia: fair and effective law enforcement and culture.	• An understanding of the impact that crime and corruption have on the culture of lawfulness • The impact of their own actions and tolerance of criminal activities on their community and society
Fostering a Culture of Lawfulness	The final section of the course was significantly revised in the current program, extensively	• Understand the role of goal setting and plan-

SECTION	DESCRIPTION	EXPECTED OUTCOMES
	detailing each of the stages of problem-solving. Problem-solving is offered as the critical tool necessary for students to put what they have learned in the rest of the course to practice, both in their individual lives and even in leading to community change. The importance of goal-setting in their lives returns students to the foundations laid in the first section of the course, teaching them to look beyond immediate gratification and jumping directly from problem to response. Instead, students are shown the importance of critically analyzing issues before developing action responses. Exercises return to students' responses in a section one exercise, "Who Am I?" with the different focus of "Who Do I Want to Be?" Problem solving is introduced as a tool to help students get there, hopefully with an invigorated sense of social responsibility resulting from participation in the course to this point.	ning in affecting change in both their own lives and the community • An understanding of how to foster a culture of lawfulness should also be reflected in the recognition that crime can be overcome, and that the community also plays a role in such efforts in collaboration with law enforcement

Key Findings from the Second Baja, California Evaluation

As expected, students showed a significantly less fatalistic world view following participation in the course. For example, 65% recognized that a person themselves is to blame if they are not a success in life, compared to 59% at outset. Importantly, a shift in student perceptions towards an internal locus of control (i.e. perception that they can influence the world around them) was also witnessed. Although locus of control was significantly correlated with academic achievement, the most dramatic changes following the course were found in those reporting poor scores. Participating students were far more likely to view each person as responsible for their actions. A small, but significant change was also evident in student self-esteem.

Students were significantly more able to recognize the elements of rule of law and a culture of lawfulness at post-testing; a corresponding increase in social responsibility was also notable on key items. For example, by course end 51% of students disagreed that they "do not owe their community anything", compared to 46% at pre-testing. As with locus of control, the most significant changes were witnessed in students performing poorly academically.

Disappointing results were found related to the obligation to obey the law and legal reasoning scales, both measuring orientation towards the law. Neither of these demonstrated significant changes. However, it may be that more time is needed developing problem-solving skills and engaging in moral dilemmas to truly see change on these items, as suggested by the empirical literature outlined in chapter two. This proposition is supported by the fact that effects were most pronounced amongst Tecate students, where teachers brought a lot of creativity and time to the problem solving lessons, as related to this study's researcher in student and teacher focus groups. Additionally, the obligation scale is a proxy for legitimacy and shown in previous studies to be significantly related to perceptions of the effectiveness of law enforcement (Tyler, 1990). However, students actually rated police fairness and effectiveness weaker following the program, perhaps reflecting a more realistic appraisal of the situation. Importantly, at post-testing significantly more students reported that they would support the police if they followed the rule of law. Finally, students were significantly more likely to appreciate the need for the community, law enforcement, and government to work together to address crime and corruption, essential ingredients in contributing to a culture of lawfulness. Not surprisingly, students did not change their peer associations within the timeframe of participation.

The combination of the above findings indicates some support for the theoretical assumptions of this study. After participation in the Culture of Lawfulness program, in which student's are challenged to assess their role in society, the nature of their associations and values, and the importance of rules and laws, some significant changes related to locus of control, social responsibility and fatalism were noted. Students also noted that they would support the police if they were to follow the rule of law. The fact that support for the police did not change positively, might be another reason why there was not significant movement in legal reasoning and obligation to obey the law, in addition to the factors noted above. The fact that changes were found related to student sense of social responsibility, but not legal reasoning, may indicate more independence between these factors than hypothesized in this study. Chapters six and seven will examine this issue further with the results of the structural equation modeling (SEM).

Overview of the Legal Context in Mexico

With a population of 103.5 million people, Mexico is a large federal democracy including one federal district (Districto Federal – DF) and 31 states. As with any country of such size and population, it is difficult to characterize its legal culture into simplistic "black and white" terms. Rather its criminal justice system, much like the United States involves a complex variety of law enforcement functions and applications that varies significantly from jurisdiction to jurisdiction. In describing the legal context of Mexico, this study will use the criteria offered by Cohn and White (1990): role of authority, fairness of enforcement, and the legitimacy of rules.

Role of authority:

When one tries to describe the political and legal culture of Mexico, many of us very succinctly try to characterize its government as a clear example of the authoritarian model; this is hardly surprising given the centralization of the executive branch in the power of the presidency, and the decades of one-party rule under the Partido Revolucionario Institucional (PRI). However, given that its 1917 constitution (at least on paper) offers many of the protections common to more advanced democracies, and the term of any one leader is limited to a six year term, many political scholars classify it as a semi-authoritarian model (Camp, 1999). Camp (1999) claims that "Mexico's unique authoritarianism sets it apart from many others" in that it allows greater access to the decision-making process, changes leaders frequently, and exhibits some characteristics of political liberalism with its constitutional principles of "social justice" (Camp, pg. 9). Some authors referred to Mexico's past model of government as:

> A perfect dictatorship disguised in democracy's costume. It is a chameleon-like regime able to present itself in left, center, or right wing ideological colors, as required by the historic moment. It is a political creature that changes faces every six years, keeping its despotic heart intact and beating strong (Galindo, 2000).

However, on July 2nd, 2000, 71 years of one party rule came to an end with the election of conservative Vincente Fox, reflecting Mexican civic society's final disgruntlement with an administration that was incapable of meeting the social needs of its huge population or making a dent in the culture of corruption that lined the pockets of politicians, police officers, and other government officials throughout the country (Ibid). Fox's promise of democratic and fiscal reform struck a chord with the voting public that hopefully will not be reversed, no matter how successful his administration is at overcoming the uphill battle that is reform in Mexico.

Even before this turnaround in Mexican politics, the Zedillo administration had made some significant strides in releasing some of the powers and impunity of the Executive Branch to Congress. By 1998, a majority of Mexicans actually viewed the Congress as more indispensable to the functioning of government than the presidency (Camp, pg. 12). Such movement, in addition to the greater freedoms provided the press, will not easily be reversed with any future administration. Journalists will no longer be afraid to criticize the actions of government, and citizens will hopefully be increasingly more likely to demand a system that is closer to the letter of some of the principals of its 1917 Constitution. The last decade thus exhibits significant changes in the role of authority in Mexico that holds the hope of an increasingly participatory civic society. However, as the case studies of Palermo and Hong Kong illustrate, such cultural shifts will not be a process that will occur overnight, and will instead require the nurturing of all sectors of society. For example, Mexicans continue to believe that overcoming poverty is more important than their political freedoms, a factor that plays a tremendous role in the nature of their demands on the political leadership; for many Mexicans, "democracy does not incorporate tolerance of opposing viewpoints" (Camp, pg.7).

Fairness of enforcement:

On both the federal and state levels, the police in Mexico are divided into the policia judicial (judicial police) and policia preventiva (preventive police), each with complementary enforcement responsibilities. The latter police branch is largely responsible for order maintenance activities throughout the cities and towns of the country; whereas, the judicial police are the investigative arm of the Public Ministry, including police officers, public prosecutor investigators, and technical experts (Reames, pg. 3). As with the United States, the nature and type of law enforcement in Mexico varies across federal, state, and local (municipal) levels, with more than 350,000 officers countrywide and around 3000 different forces across all levels (Ibid).

The fact that in 1999 90% of Mexico City residents responded that they have little to no trust in the police is hardly surprising in the context of the history of inefficiency, corruption, and civil rights violations that have characterized policing in the country. Reames (2004) reports that a 2002 advocacy group estimated that "the median Mexican household spends 8% of its income on bribes, ranking 57th in Transparency International's global scale of the perception of corruption (pg. 5). Within this context of corruption, overall crime rates continued to increase significantly throughout the previous decade, increasing general citizen concern about public insecurity. Much of the corruption that occurs in positions of power within Mexico has historically been related to the narcotics industry (Reding, 1995). Moreover, the involved cabinet-level officials engaging in these acts have generally operated in impunity given an unwritten rule forbidding the prosecution of ministers (Ibid). According to Reding (1995), this impunity has traditionally left anyone willing to take a public stance against corruption at a considerable risk for state-sanctioned acts of retributive violence.

The criminal justice system itself proved susceptible to the threats of organized crime and corruption in that "through intimidation, coercion, and bribery of judges, major criminals (have had) serious charges dismissed, allowing them back on the street to continue their criminal activities" (Pimental, 2000). The impunity of both criminals and corrupt officials has played a major role in deteriorating the confidence of civil society. Without major reforms in the professionalism and transparency of law enforcement, allowing its actions to be open to public scrutiny, there will continue to be a lack of trust in the Mexican law enforcement authorities (Ibid.). Legislative reforms designed to facilitate the process of combating organized crime and corruption similar to the actions described above in Palermo will also play a significant role in restoring legitimacy.

Inaction related to the problem of drug trafficking is not the only source of problems related to the legitimacy of the overall legal culture. In fact, the "war on drugs" has itself led to serious human rights abuses, particularly by the federal narcotics police (Americas Watch, 1990). Despite serious attempts to reform law enforcement practices by the Fox administration, including a willingness to acknowledge a problem, murder, torture, and other due process abuses continue to exist. In the past, officers of the "Federal Police's anti-narcotics division (have) routinely committed acts far worse than those they are trying to stop" (Americas Watch, pg. 4).

A recent report prepared by Pro Juarez (2001) along with the Lawyers Committee for Human Rights notes that not only do human rights violations continue to occur in Mexico, the particularly disturbing fact is that in many respects they are "legal" through either explicit sanctions or loose interpretations of Mexican Law. "While all violations of the law tend to undermine its credibility, when the law permits or rationalizes actions which should be understood as clearly illegal, and converts them into the 'normal' by product of the legal process, the damage is even greater" (Juarez, pg.1). Among the practices contributing to continued human rights violations, Pro Juarez (2001) cites:

- wide allowances for warrantless arrests that allow police the discretion to make arrests without judicial oversight;
- the practice of detaining individuals for weeks without officially registering their custody, allowing for the practices of abuse and torture to elicit confessions;
- despite legal provisions against the admittance into court of confessions given in the absence of counsel, in practice suspects can be detained and interrogated for days by police without counsel;
- coerced confessions continue to be admitted as evidence by judges even where there is significant evidence suggesting coercion; and,
- a lack of independence between judges, prosecutors, and the executive branch.

In addition to all of the above enabling conditions, there continues to be reluctance on the part of appellate courts to overturn appeals on the basis of police or prosecutorial practices (Ibid.). Finally, the military continues to play a major role in Mexican law enforcement, despite constitutional provisions against such practices.

The combination of due process violations and corrupt practices involved in Mexican law enforcement no doubt go a long way towards fostering a lack of faith in the legal system amongst Mexicans. Moreover, many of the above violations are far more prevalent amongst the lower classes and ethnic minorities. Evictions of peasant families have been known to occur without warning and violence against minority groups by the state often go unpunished. Remembering that making sub-groups feel connected to the larger national identity is an important component of legitimacy should illustrate to the reader just how difficult building a citizenry that respects the rule of law and has a related sense of social responsibility will be in Mexico, given the legacy of violations it has to overcome (Lind, Kray and Thompson 2001; Tyler, 2000).

Legitimacy of rules:

Given the combination of these factors, it is hardly surprising that when Mexicans are asked to evaluate their societal institutions, those more closely associated with the powers of the state are viewed most negatively (Camp, pg. 54). For example, Camp (1999) reports a 1988 public opinion survey which found that 88% of Americans gave a positive evaluation of the police and 83% supported the activities of Congress; this is in contrast to 12% of Mexicans viewing the police positively, and 39% seeing the actions of Congress as legitimate (Ibid). In contrast, throughout history Mexicans have viewed the institutions of church and family as being the prime source of legitimate socialization. While these sectors are also held in high regard in American society, they are balanced with the powers of state and law enforcement. Of course, such a statement needs to be interpreted cautiously given the known variation across different communities and demographics within the United States (Jones Brown, 1996).

<u>Summary</u>

The theoretical basis for the culture of lawfulness approach has its origins in countries as diverse as Hong Kong and Palermo, Sicily. As with the basic tenets of the community policing movement, there is a recognition that even serious crimes involving organized crime and corruption require the collaboration of multiple sectors of society, including law enforcement, schools, churches, business, and the media.

When societies operate in serious violation of the rule of law, as is the case in the legacy of Mexican law enforcement practices, the general population is much more likely to overestimate the powers of government, and feel a sense of helplessness in relation to the political order. Although institutions such as the family and church can play a countering positive force for socialization in such societies, it will not be enough to stimulate the belief in the principles of fairness and justice characteristic of a postconventional belief in the rule of law.

In the Hong Kong and Sicilian case studies provided in this chapter there was a catalyst that finally pushed the citizenry to demand change – reinvigorating a formerly challenged sense of social responsibility.

Although without such a dramatic beginning, the Culture of Lawfulness project's origins in Tijuana, Mexico and the U.S. side of the border was in response to a group of teachers finally having enough of the criminogenic conditions that were wreaking havoc in the lives of their students. Based upon the Hong Kong and Sicilian examples a course was developed that is theoretically based upon the legal socialization principles that is the core of this study.

The legal context of Mexico presents numerous challenges in terms of fostering a culture of lawfulness in the face of a legacy of human rights abuses and formerly semi-authoritarian rule. However, returning to Orlando's analogy of the two wheeled cart, there are now enough positive signs in Mexican government to be hopeful. There has been a tremendous change in the powers of the executive branch, an increasing willingness to acknowledge the human rights violations of law enforcement and push for change, and an increasing transparency of governmental actions embodied in freedoms to the press. Once such progress has been made, it becomes very difficult for future administrations to reverse. Witnessing such developments, civic society will be increasingly more likely to demand the type of government and law enforcement that it deserves. It is argued that all of these factors will have a bearing on general levels of legal reasoning, and in turn, lawful behavior.

CHAPTER FIVE

Research Methodology

"In the legal socialization theory, it is believed that youths' feelings of closeness to authority figures, their assessment of the authority figure's legitimacy, and their assessment of the legitimacy of the juvenile justice institution influence the impact of experiences on legal reasoning (Morash, 1978: 70)".

Introduction

The hypotheses to be tested in this study relate to the pattern of causal structure linking selected risk factors from the criminological literature (i.e. peer delinquency, perceptions of safety, attitudes toward school, locus of control) in addition to perceptions of police legitimacy, to bear on the construct of legal reasoning. In turn, the impact of legal reasoning on self-reported delinquency (through the attitudinal mediators of obligation to the law and social responsibility) is also examined.

This study is part of a larger evaluation of the Culture of Lawfulness program throughout the state of Baja California, Mexico described in chapter 4. Although the evaluation study utilized a pre-post test design, the current study is cross-sectional, developing the empirical pathway across only the pre-test data. Future studies can examine the degree to which exposure to the curriculum alters the pathway documented in the current study.

<u>Research Objectives for the Current Study</u>

This study seeks to examine the possible theoretical and empirical linkages between the legal socialization, procedural justice, and resiliency literatures. As such, ten variables have been selected from the Mexican Culture of Lawfulness pre-test instrument with theoretical importance to each of these areas:

- Drawing from the legal socialization literature, the study will include a measure of **legal reasoning (LR)**, or the way in which study respondents interpret information related to the importance and necessity of rules and laws in society.

- Three variables from the procedural justice literature have been selected as measures of respondent perceptions of legitimacy. The first, **support for the police (SPol)** measures respondent perceptions of the fairness of law enforcement. The second variable, **obligation to obey the law (O),** is an attitudinal measure of the extent to which respondents view the law as deserving of respect and worth compliance. Both of these variables were originally a part of the larger efforts of Tom Tyler (1990), as described below. A third variable, **social responsibility (SR)** measures the degree of commitment (or "citizenship") each youth feels towards his or her community in terms of responsibility to contribute to its well-being.

- Variables have been selected from four of the five risk factor domains discussed in chapter three. Individual risk factor variables include **self-esteem (SE)** and **locus of control (LC)**. The **peers (P)** variable measures the degree to which an individual associates with positive and negative influences. The **personal safety (PS)** variable examines perceptions of respondents' safety within the community risk factor domain. Finally, **attitudes towards school (AS)** measure youth attachment to school, a central variable within the school risk factor domain.

Figure 2 Conceptual Model of Study Hypotheses

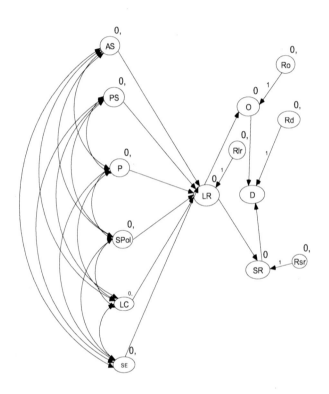

Prior to providing the reader with further details related to the structure, reliability, and validity of each of the scales used to measure these ten variables, Figure-2 provides a conceptual model of the hypothesized relationships between the study variables that will be assessed in the remainder of this work. The model leads from risk factors empirically demonstrated to influence delinquency (attitudes toward school, perceptions of safety, peer delinquency, locus of control, self-esteem) and perceptions of police fairness (legitimacy factor one) to legal reasoning.

Having a low self-esteem and external locus of control has often surfaced in empirical studies as potentially increasing an individual's likelihood of becoming involved in delinquent or other problem behaviors (Tiet and Huizinga, 2002; Werner, 1994). Both of these variables are classified as internal risk factors, in that they are more related to individual than external characteristics; however, the procedural justice literature has noted that both of these variables may be influenced by an unfair or oppressive legal context as well (Tyler, 2000). Not having adequate feelings of self-worth, or feeling helpless to influence one's environment (external locus of control) will make an individual less likely to engage in the social interaction and role-taking activities empirically demonstrated to advance legal reasoning (Tapp and Levine 1977; Tapp and Levine, 1974).

Similarly, a community environment that is perceived as unsafe or violent can also lead to a perception of helplessness that discourages role-taking activities. Moreover, such a community context does not provide youths with sufficient models related to the importance (or even utility) of rules and laws in society. As such, these conditions are hypothesized to have a retarding effect on legal reasoning, making an individual view families or peers as more important controls of conduct than the formal rule-enforcing context (Finkenaur, 1995). Such conditions will be exacerbated by the negative influences of delinquent peers, such as those involved in gangs or other criminal activities. Peer interactions have been identified as the most important type of social role-taking activities for moral reasoning advancement in many studies (Sedikides, 1989).

Finally, the influence of the overall legal or rule-enforcing context is also hypothesized to impact legal reasoning development as a result of the available role-taking opportunities and general models for conduct provided. Support for the police, as indicated by a belief in their fairness, has often been demonstrated to influence delinquency justifications in youths (Brown, 1974; Jones Brown, 2000). It is proposed that a belief in the unfairness of police practice may retard legal reasoning because it demonstrates the futility of the rule of law in practice, making individuals less likely to develop the justice or human rights orientation characteristic of level three postconventional rule-making thought.

Put more simply, legal reasoning has been conceptualized as a potential "resiliency" factor that is affected (i.e. retarded or advanced) by different combinations of these identified exogenous variables, at the same time as it can potentially "mediate" their relationships with youth delinquency.

Other studies have shown the importance of attitudinal mediators in the causal structure between legal reasoning and behavior (Cohn and White, 1990). Obligation to obey the law (legitimacy factor two) and social responsibility are suggested as key attitudinal mediators that are influenced by an individual's level of legal reasoning, and that, in turn, impact his or her overall rate of delinquent activities. For example, higher levels of legal reasoning are expected to cause increased social responsibility, and a corresponding decline in delinquent conduct due to an increased likelihood to feel a need to act in the interest of one's community or society generally.

Primary Hypotheses:

The primary hypotheses deal with the observed relationship between legal culture (legitimacy of police), legal reasoning level, attitudinal measures of legitimacy (obligation to obey the law and social responsibility), and finally self-reported delinquent behavior. These have been expressed in the six following hypotheses:

Hypothesis 1: Higher support for the police (legitimacy factor-1) has a positive causal effect on the legal reasoning level of youths;

Hypothesis 2: Higher legal reasoning levels will, in turn, have a positive causal effect on obligation to obey the law (legitimacy factor-2) and social responsibility;

Hypothesis 3: Greater obligation to obey the law and social responsibility will have a negative causal effect on self-reported delinquent behavior.

Hypothesis 4: The effect of support for the police on obligation to obey the law and social responsibility is mediated through legal reasoning.

Hypothesis 5: The effect of support for the police on delinquency is mediated through legal reasoning; and,

Hypothesis 6: The effect of legal reasoning on delinquency is mediated through the attitudes of obligation to obey the law and social responsibility.

Secondary Hypotheses:

The causes of exogenous variables are not represented in path models (Kline, 1998). Given the current study's efforts to establish the empirical linkages between legitimacy theories, legal development theory, and resiliency theory, four exogenous variables were selected to measure aspects of each of these domains: delinquent peers, locus of control, self-esteem, and attachment to school. There is an assumed unanalyzed association between these exogenous variables as demonstrated by the curved arrows. Each variable is hypothesized to have some potential retarding effect on legal development level:

Hypothesis 7: Having delinquent peers will have a negative causal effect on legal reasoning;

Hypothesis 8: Having a low self-esteem will have a negative causal effect on legal reasoning;

Hypothesis 9: Having an external locus of control will have a negative causal effect on legal reasoning;

Hypothesis 10: Having poor school attachment will have a negative causal effect on legal reasoning; and,

Hypothesis 11: The effects of each of the exogenous variables (i.e. peers, self-esteem, locus of control, and attitudes toward school) on obligation to obey the law and social responsibility will be mediated through legal reasoning; and,

Hypothesis 12: The effects of each of the exogenous variables (i.e. peers, self-esteem, locus of control, and attitudes toward school) on delinquency will be mediated through legal reasoning.

As indicated by hypotheses 5-6 and 11-12, secondary analysis will examine the extent to which legal reasoning can "mediate" the negative effects of these exogenous variables. Residual variables have been included to allow for the fact that the predictor variables in the model do not fully account for the values of each of the endogenous variables (i.e. legal reasoning, obligation to obey the law, social responsibility, and delinquency).

<u>Sampling and Data Collection Procedures</u>

Over ten thousand (N=10,437) Mexican youths from throughout Baja, California (Tijuana, MexiCali, Tecate, and Ensenada) responded to the pre-test survey in September 2001 prior to beginning the jointly sponsored State Education System/NSIC school-based curriculum to counter crime and corruption described in chapter four. All youths were secundaria students in the United States equivalent of ninth grade. Secundaria is the last point in the Mexican "basic education cycle"; "after secundaria, students must choose between several different options, including college preparatories, vocational schools, business courses, and secretarial or cosmetological schools" (Levinson, 2001, pg. 7).

Although the sample represents a significant proportion of the ninth grade secundaria population in Baja California at the time of the study, it must be stressed that this is a non-probability convenience sample of only the universe of students participating in the Culture of Lawfulness program. It is important to note that there is a significant drop out rate between the first and third years of secundaria in Mexico, requiring caution in generalizing study results to all Mexican youths between the ages of 14 and 15 (Levinson, 2001). It is likely that many of the more seriously non-conforming youths will no longer have been enrolled in school, and thus unavailable for participation in both the Culture of Lawfulness program and thus the study reported here. The extent to which Mexican students differ by the various options available in the "basic education cycle" (i.e. secundaria general, secundaria tecnica, and telesecundaria) is not known. Again, the current sample represents the vast majority of ninth grade secundaria students participating in the Baja California Culture of Lawfulness program. Figure-3 describes the major options and paths in Mexican schooling. The administration of the pre-tests was coordinated jointly between staff at the National Strategy Information Center (NSIC) and Culture of Lawfulness program coordinators in each of the participating Baja municipalities. Pre-testing occurred throughout the first week of September, 2001.[6] In all cases, the principal spoke to the students (either in an assembly or in individual classes) to introduce the class and the NSIC representative.[7] The NSIC representative discussed the nature of the survey and its relationship to the class the students were about to take. NSIC staff always stressed that students were not taking a test and that their responses were totally anonymous. These same instructions are on the top of each survey as shown in appendices A and B. Proctors were available during the administration of the instrument (from both NSIC and the State Education System) to assist students should the need arise. In no case was the same teacher that would be teaching the culture of lawfulness curriculum present during this process. Following the administration of the test, the NSIC representative would count all answer sheets and returned instruments, sign a document indicating the count, and seal them in an envelope that was shipped to the NSIC office in Washington, DC. The data was scanned into an SPSS compatible format using SCANTRON technology, and later made available to the author of this study.

---

[6] Post-testing took place throughout the first week of June, 2002. However, as this study only utilized the pre-test data for analysis, all further discussion of the data collection process will only refer to the September phase of the larger evaluation study.

[7] The author served in this capacity for all schools in Tecate and Ensenada.

Figure 3 Major Options and Paths in Mexican Schooling

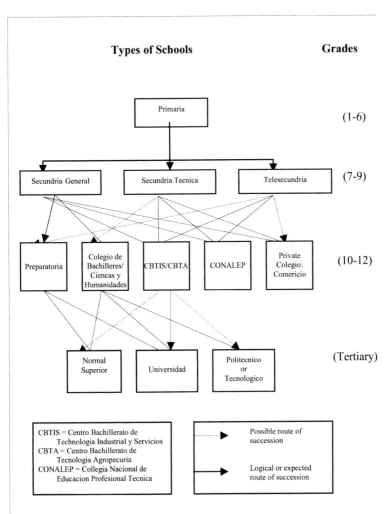

Source: Levinson, B. (2001). *We Are All Equal: Student Culture and Identity at a Mexican Secondary School.* Durham: Duke University Press.

Research Instrument and Variables

For the 2001 Baja, California evaluation, an instrument was developed including 97 questions, with 11 theoretically-derived sub-scales: attitudes toward school, personal safety, fatalism, social responsibility, locus of control, self-esteem, obligation to obey the law, support for the police, legal reasoning, self-reported delinquency, and peer associations. In addition, the instrument includes 19 substantive knowledge questions related to the content of the lessons covered in the curriculum to assess changes in student knowledge as a result of participation in the course. The Spanish version actually used with the study's respondents is included in Appendix A. The English version of the instrument in its entirety is included in Appendix B.

In accordance with the causal structure indicated by the hypotheses outlined above, the current research project will use all of the scales except for the substantive knowledge questions and fatalism scale. Each of the scales being utilized will be briefly described below in this section. As the instrument represents a composite of scales from research only conducted in the United States, and was translated for the first time into the Spanish language, significant attention will be paid to its validation below.

Reliability/Validity of the Chosen Sub-scales:

In selecting the sub-scales for the instrument, the researcher sought previously published, standardized measures that could reliably assess student attitudes, behaviors, and knowledge. Following completion of instrument selection and development, a Spanish-speaking NSIC staff member translated the instrument into Spanish. Table-4 summarizes the sub-scales being used in this study and their reliability.

All of the reliability information pertains only to the targeted groups on which they were measured. Two of the scales (i.e. personal safety and self-esteem) were tested on large samples of middle school students. One scale (i.e. Attitudes toward schools) used adolescent African-American males to assess reliability. Finally, the locus of control, obligation, and support for the police scales were tested on large diverse populations in Chicago (9, 325 and 1, 575 respectively).

Table 4 Scales comprising the *Mexican Culture of Lawfulness Inventory* and their sources.

Variables	Scale	Reliability	Author
Attachment to school	Attitudes Toward School – Denver Youth Survey	Internal consistency α=.38 AA males: 12-16	Institute of Behavioral Science, 1990
Personal safety	Personal Safety – Joyce Foundation Youth Survey	Internal consistency α=.63 Middle school: 6-8	LH Research, Inc., 1993
Locus of control	Locus of control and Attribution Style Test – R	Internal consistency α=: .80 Adult and adolescent population – 9,325	Jerabek, 2000
Self-esteem	Modified Rosenberg's Self-Esteem Scale	Internal consistency α=.50 Middle school: 6-8	Rosenberg, 1965
Obligation to obey the law	Obligation	Internal consistency α=.79	Tyler, 1990
Perceptions of police fairness	Support for the police	Internal consistency α=.81 to .85	Tyler, 1990
Legal reasoning	Legal Reasoning Scale	Internal consistency α=: .77	Tapp and Levine, 1974
Social responsibility	Responsibility and Citizenship Scale	Internal consistency α=: .52	Nedwek, 1987
Self-reported non-conforming behavior	Involvement in Deviant Acts	Not available	Gottfredson, 1991
Delinquent peers	Friend's Delinquent Behavior – Adolescent Attitude Survey	Internal consistency α=.86	Center for Urban Affairs and Policy Research

Overall instrument parsimony had to be taken into consideration during the selection process given the short two-hour time frame available for instrument administration. As noted above, with respect to the current study, the entire instrument needed to be revalidated given that none of the above reliability assessments were conducted on a population of Mexican adolescents. The validation of the study instrument involved the collaboration of a colleague of the author. Although major findings will be described in this section related to the variables included in the current study (i.e. legal reasoning, support for the police, obligation, locus of control, self-esteem, peer associations, personal safety, social responsibility, and self-reported delinquency), an additional paper is available for information (Rengifo, 2003). In addition to the calculation of the internal consistency of each of the scales using Chronbach alpha, an exploratory factor analysis (EFA) was conducted using the direct oblimin factor rotation.

Legal Reasoning

Legal reasoning is the core construct being measured in the current study. This eleven-item scale remains the same as that used during the pilot evaluation to measure the students' conceptions of rules, laws, rights and responsibilities (Godson and Kenney, 2000). Based on the principles of the Tapp-Kohlberg-Levine model of legal socialization, these questions present students with statements reflecting the three levels of legal reasoning detailed above: preconventional, conventional, and postconventional. Questions cover such issues as the reasons for individual rights, the circumstances under which laws can be changed, and the justifications for rule or law violation.

For each of the eleven items, a score of 1 is offered for the preconventional response, 2 for the conventional response, and three for the post-conventional response. A maximum score on legal reasoning items would thus be 33 if the respondent answered post-conventionally to all items. An average of scores across the three levels thereby results in a score on a continuum between 1 and 3, giving a general picture of respondent overall reasoning (Tapp and Levine, 1974). Finckenauer (1995) and Jones Brown (1996) piloted the close ended version of this scale used in this study, finding it had a significant reliability measure of .77.

Possibly as the result of some translation issues with some of the scale items, the initial reliability estimate was found to be very poor, yielding an alpha estimator of .06. An examination of the scale's inter-item correlations indicated that several of the items were negatively correlated that should not be based on the theoretical underpinnings of the instrument, thereby decreasing its overall validity. After eliminating those items that were negatively correlated with the others, the EFA of the scale items revealed three factors in the scale, only one with enough consistency (α=.39) to be included in the current scale. Importantly, the remaining four item construct also represented the most theoretically "solid" items in the judgment of the researcher. See Table-5 for a summary of indicators left in the study (for legal reasoning and all other scales used). Obviously, future research should seek to develop a more reliable and valid measure of the legal reasoning construct.

Legitimacy Variables

Both the obligation and support for the police sub-scales were derived from Tyler's (1990) large scale study in Chicago of randomly selected citizens to assess the normative factors involved in compliance with the law, and the impact of experiences on the perceived legitimacy of legal authorities. These two sub-scales include 12-items, with high scores on support for the police (four item scale with a highest possible score of 14) measuring perceptions of fairness and police legitimacy and a high score on obligation indicated a greater sense of obligation to obey the law. In both cases, scores are divided by the total number of possible items to provide a final index on the variable of interest.

    a) Support for the Police.

On two of the "support for the police" items, respondents indicate how often police offer "good" services with "fair" outcomes (i.e. rarely, sometimes, often, always). The remaining two items ask the respondent to evaluate the overall performance of the police and whether or not they feel they favor some people over others. Importantly, NSIC added a fifth "don't know" category to the instrument which presented challenges to the researcher given that it was not theoretically based.

For the purposes of this study, respondent evaluations of the police were essential whether or not they are based upon personal experience or not. As such, the "don't know" response category was re-coded as missing. Because the number of "don't know" responses across the two items was significant (representing 28.5% of the sample on one item and 14.1% on the other), the researcher compared the covariance matrices of the two groups to determine whether or not the youths who had a clear perception of the police were statistically significantly different than those who did not. The results of this multi-group analysis indicated that there was not a significant difference, thereby allowing the researcher to conduct all study analyses assuming one sample (as opposed to two).

As both the alpha measure for internal consistency (α=.62) was adequate, and the EFA determined that all four support for the police items were loading on one factor, all items were kept in the study as indicators of the "support for the police" construct. The "support for the police" construct is an exogenous variable in the hypothesized model.

b) Obligation to Obey the Law

The "obligation" items (8 items with a highest possible score of 36) examine willingness to obey the law, even in circumstances where one might disagree with the outcome. As with the "support for the police" scale, respondents are offered four possible response options, ranging from "strongly agree" to "strongly disagree". After removing four items following the EFA, a four-item scale remained for this study (see Table-5) that all loaded on the "obligation" latent construct and had a reliability estimate of .45. "Obligation" is hypothesized as one of two "attitudinal mediators" between legal reasoning and self-reported delinquency.

Selected Risk Factors

Ideally the study's exogenous variables would include at least one measure from each of the domains described in chapter three (individual, family, peer, school, and community). However, as the NSIC instrument does not include any items from within the family domain, this will have to be the subject of future research.

a) Individual Domain

Locus of Control. The locus of control indicators were modified from the 33 question Locus of Control and Attribution Style Test (Jerabek, 2000) to include eleven items. Modifications were made solely in the interest of keeping the number of total items in the instrument to a manageable level to be completed in the allotted two hour time period. Those items most aligned with the content of the curriculum being evaluated in the original evaluation context were kept. Low scores indicate an external locus of control, and high scores represent an internal locus of control. As discussed above, locus of control refers to an individual's belief about the causes of certain outcomes, including rewards and punishments (Bandura, 1975; Rotter, 1954), making its potential impact on legal reasoning very clear.

Individuals with an internal locus of control orientation feel that they have a tremendous degree of control over their own lives and can influence its outcomes. On the opposite end of the spectrum, an external orientation places tremendous weight on external factors controlling one's life, such as luck or fate. As such, the 11 indicators included in the instrument ask respondents to rate the degree to which they are responsible for their actions and goal attainment (i.e. through a four-item response range to statements ranging from "completely agree" to "completely disagree").

Interestingly, given the legal context of Mexico, one of the indicators that proved to be especially problematic (i.e. with negative correlations with all other items) was, "I can complain about politics but that is all I can do". It may be that given the political situation in the country, one could both have an internal locus of control and still strongly agree with this statement. The results of the EFA revealed that the locus of control items loaded on three factors, only one of which maintained high internal consistency with an α estimator of .74, thereby reducing the original 11 item scale to four strong items.

Self-esteem. These four items from the Modified Rosenberg (1989) measure respondent self-esteem with respect to attention at home, popularity at school, desire to be a different person, and post-school chances for successes. High scores indicate higher self-esteem, with response items to a series of statements ranging from "strongly disagree" to "strongly agree". The "self-esteem" scale demonstrated the second poorest internal consistency of the entire scale with an α of .27. After removing the most problematic inter-item correlation of .08, the α estimator for the remaining three items used in this study was only able to be strengthened to a high of .30. Future research may wish to use a more valid and reliable measure of self-esteem, possibly returning to the larger Rosenberg (1989) scale upon which the current scale is based.

b) Peer Domain

The Friend's Delinquent Behavior – Adolescent Attitude Survey (Center for Urban Affairs and Policy Research, 1995) is a seven-item scale that measures the number of positive and negative associations a student has had in the 60 days prior to the survey; higher scores indicate greater exposure to friends who engage in socially acceptable behavior. The positive items in the scale (i.e. asking whether or not their friends had encouraged them to stop a fight, go to church, or complete their homework) posed the greatest threats to its internal consistency. Given the strong emphasis on religion in Mexican culture, the fact that "going to church" is not particularly discriminating between positive and negative associations is not very surprising. It may be that churchgoing behaviors are equally likely amongst both delinquent and nondelinquents youths. After removing these positive oriented items (keeping the items relating to breaking the law, vandalism, gang activities, and hitting somebody), the α estimator for consistency in the four remaining items was .70.

c) School Domain

This five item scale measures "attachment to school" through a series of statements in which respondents state the degree to which they agree across a four-point scale from "completely disagree" to "completely agree". High scores equate with increased attachment to school. Analyses of scale internal consistency revealed that removing the item "I don't care what my teachers think about me" could increase the scale internal consistency to an α of .39 (from .25), making the "attachment to school" measure in this study four items.

d) Community Domain

Personal Safety. This four-item sub-scale (LH Research, Inc., 1993) measures the presence of gangs and violence in the neighborhood and school setting. Each question offers the respondent a chance to rate the degree to which they worry about their safety in their neighborhood on a five-point scale ranging from "always" to "never". High scores indicate perceptions of less safety in the student's contextual environment. In this case, only one item posed a problem and had to be removed from the scale for this study: "I observe gang activity in my neighborhood". In addition to the fact that Rengifo (2003) notes the item was translated as "see" in Spanish rather than observe, this item does not go well with the others on even a face validity level. The other three items specifically address respondent concerns about their safety in the neighborhood or going to and from school. The presence of gangs, however, may be interpreted as positive or something that does not concern them at all, causing the item to not load well with the others. Removing this item from the scale increased the α estimator for the four remaining items to .57.

Social Responsibility

The five-items measuring "social responsibility" ask respondents the degree to which they agree or disagree with statements about their expectations in life and relationship to their communities using a five-point scale ranging from "strongly agree" to "strongly disagree". One of the items ("I truly care how my actions affect other people") had to be eliminated due to extremely low correlations with the other items of the scale as confirmed by the EFA. Interestingly, the one item removed from the "attachment to school" scale ("I don't care what my teachers think about me") was shown to load on this scale in the EFA. This can likely be explained by the fact that strong attachment to teachers is a reflection of bonds with the one socialization actor students are exposed to as much as (or in some cases, more than) their parents. Consequently, this item was added to this scale in the current study, and the problematic item described above was removed. The revised "social responsibility" scale has an α of .49.

Self-Reported Delinquency

To allow for comparison with the pilot project, the same 6-items used to measure "self-reported delinquency" were replicated (Godson and Kenney, 2000), measuring deviance ranging from avoiding paying for bus rides to robbery or serious violence. Similar to the "peer associations" measure described above, respondents are asked to report the frequency of their delinquent activity over the previous 60 days on a continuum ranging from minor activities to significantly violent offenses. High scores on this item mean greater frequency of self-reported delinquency. This measure behaved as well as expected, with the EFA confirming that all of its items load significantly on the same factor, and that there is adequate internal consistency with an α estimator of .74.

Table 5 Summary Table of remaining scale items and internal consistency

SCALE	REMAINING ITEMS INCLUDED IN STUDY	α
Legal reasoning	V58. People should have rights that: V59. It must be right to break a law when: V62. A law can be changed when: V63. People can be right and break the law when:	.39
Support for the police	V42:Overall, how good is the performance of the police? Are they doing....... V43:Some people say that the police deal with everybody the same way; other people think they	

SCALE	REMAINING ITEMS INCLUDED IN STUDY	α
	favor some people over other. What do you think? V44:If you ask the police for help, how often would they offer a good service? V45:When citizens deal with the police, how often do they get fair outcomes?	.62
Obligation	V53. If a police officer asks you to stop you should stop even if you feel that what you were doing is legal. V46. People should obey the law even if it goes against what they think is right. V47. I always try to follow the law even if I think that it is wrong.	.45
Self-esteem	V38:I am as popular as other people my age. V39:I would like to be somebody else. V40:I have the attention of the people in my household.	.30
Attitudes Toward School	V7. Homework is a waste of time. V8. I try hard in school. V9. Education is so important that it is worth putting up with things about school that I don't like.	.39
Peer associations	**In the last 60 days, how many of your friends (those you usually hang around with)......** V71. .....suggested you do something that was against the law? V73. .....broke or destroyed another person's property? V75. .....were involved in gang activities? V77. .....hit or threatened to hit somebody?	.70
Social responsibility	V11: I don't care what teachers think about me. V21: It is hard to get ahead without breaking the law once in awhile. V22: If I want to get in trouble, it is my business and nobody else's. V23: I don't owe anything to my community. V24:What I decide to do with my life will not make a difference in any way.	.49
Self-reported	**In the last 60 days, how many times.....**	

SCALE	REMAINING ITEMS INCLUDED IN STUDY	α
delinquency	V65. ....you intentionally broke or destroyed another person's property? V66. ....robbed (or intended to rob) something of great value? V67. ....attacked someone with a serious intention of hurting/ killing him/her? V68. ....participated in fights? V69. ....abstained from paying for things such as movie tickets, bus fare or food? V70. ....used (repressive) force to obtain money or another person's belongings – for instance, the money of one of your schoolmates.	.70

<u>Within and Across Scales Inter-item Correlations: Instrument Power for Statistical Testing</u>

As the previous discussion demonstrates, the scales are mixed in terms of overall internal consistency or reliability. Reliability itself is a necessary, though not sufficient, determinant of the overall validity of an instrument. Increasing the reliability of a measure does not necessarily lead to a corresponding increase in its validity. Although the statistical power of the current study is uncharacteristically significant given the tremendous sample size, some of this power may be decreased somewhat due to the poor inter-item correlations within and across some of the scales. To examine the internal structure of the overall instrument, Table-6 visually displays inter-item correlations both within and across scales.

Table 6 Within and Across Scale Inter-item Correlations

INTER-ITEM CORRELATION	WITHIN SCALES	ACROSS SCALES
Above .40	20	0
.30 to .39	39	0
.20 to .29	20	0
.10 to .19	49	79

-.10 to .09	17	554
-.10 to -.19	0	37
-.20 to -.29	0	18
-.30 to -.39	0	6
Below -.40	0	0
TOTAL	145	694

Although there is no established formula for determining the desirable level of inter-item correlations, a commonly accepted standard for factor loadings is that each item load on the appropriate factor at least .3 or greater, and not have a loading of greater than .3 on any other factor (Rest et al, 1999). With respect to within scale inter-item correlations, 40.6% of the items are .3 or greater. None of our across scale inter-item correlations are greater than.3, with significantly 79.8% of the correlations being lower than + or - .10. The actual factor loadings of the remaining indicators will be presented in the following chapter in our discussion of the confirmatory factor analysis (CFA) and measurement model.

In summary, the low correlations provide us with some reason to be cautious prior to interpreting any of the results offered in the next chapter. Although the study utilizes an uncharacteristically large sample size (N=10,437), low correlations within and across scales may limit the power to distinguish between alternative models, even with a large sample.

<u>Scopes and Limitations</u>

The sheer size of the respondent population provides a great opportunity for the researcher to test the proposed causal model between support for the police, community and individual risk factors, legal reasoning, obligation to obey the law, and self-reported behavior and peer associations. However, given the age of the respondent population, and the seriousness of the delinquent acts being measured, many students vulnerable to the effects of crime and corruption at the baseline due to the exogenous study variables may not yet have engaged in significant delinquent acts or begun to associate with such peers, or not be in school as noted above. Conversely, although the survey is anonymous, increasing the likelihood of honest responses, there is still the possibility of respondent bias when answering these important behavioral and peer association measures. The original pilot evaluation picked up on very little self-reported delinquent behavior (Godson and Kenney, 2000). Descriptives of the level of delinquent behavior in this study are presented in the following chapter.

The research questions being addressed in the current study could have used a more complete and reliable assessment of the community contexts surrounding each school, possibly with archival measures of crime and census figures (i.e. demographics, median income, etc). Class has been hypothesized to play an important role in influencing support for the police by many researchers (Jones-Brown, 1996). However, the inclusion of such measures was well beyond the data collection capacity of the effort upon which the proposed study is based. Future research needs to build on this effort. The diversity in reading comprehension level of the sample is also an important issue in addressing the validity of responses. Regrettably, no such measure exists of the study respondents; although it can be sure to vary significantly across the sample given the wide variety of participating schools (e.g. urban/rural, poor/moderate, small/large, etc.). Later replications of this study need to take this variable into account; particularly since studies of recognition measures of moral reasoning have been shown to vary by reading comprehension levels (see chapter seven).

Finally, as noted above, specific attention will have to be paid to the balance between the statistical power available to this study based on the enormous sample size, and the questionable reliability of some of its items. This issue will be addressed further in the discussion chapter.

<u>Ethical Problems of the Current Study</u>

As described above, students were not asked to include their names with the submission of the pre-test, so no serious human subjects' issues are raised. Although the test was part of an overall curriculum evaluation, at no point was the same teacher present, and clear instructions (both written and oral) emphasized that there are no right or wrong answers because students were not being graded based on the instrument. The instrument includes self-reported delinquency and other potentially negative attitudes, but the survey administration is within the context of a course that will address each of the issues raised for students while completing the instrument. All results are anonymous and only analyzed on an aggregate level.

CHAPTER SIX

Results

Moral advance consists not in adapting individual natures to the fixed realities of a moral universe, but in constantly reconstructing and recreating the world as individuals evolve.
George Herbert Mead, 1908

Introduction

The previous chapters have established the theoretical explanations for the current study, as well as the practical origins of its underpinnings in locations as diverse as Hong Kong, Palermo, and Mexico. To summarize, the principal objective of the study is to assess the proposed overlap between legal socialization theory and resiliency theory by exploring the extent to which legal reasoning is affected by and mediates the criminogenic influences of selected community and individual risk factors. Additional linkages between these approaches and major efforts in the procedural justice literature are also examined.

As the study seeks to examine the causal pathways and relationships between risk/protective factors, perceptions of the police, legal reasoning, obligation/social responsibility, and behavior, structural equation modeling (SEM) is the most appropriate method of analysis. Byrne (1998) notes that SEM takes a confirmatory approach to the multivariate analysis of a structural theory influencing some phenomenon. In this case, the study examines the impact of selected risk factors on delinquency through an individual's cognitive processing related to rules and laws (legal reasoning). Moreover, SEM allows for the revealed causal associations in a study to be represented by a series of structural (i.e. regression) equations, and these structural equations can be modeled graphically to allow a clear conceptualization of the theoretical associations being studied. It is important to stress, however, that because the data used in this study is cross-sectional, the direction of causality cannot be inferred from the results of the study (Shadish, Cook, and Campbell, 2002).

The large sample (N=10,437) of Mexican youths is significantly greater than the minimum sample size requirements for SEM. For example, some authors have referred to 200 as being the "critical sample size" (Hair, Anderson, Tatham, and Black, 1999), whereas others have noted that SEM requires the ratio of participants to parameters to be at least 10:1 (Kline, 1998).

<u>Demographics of the Study Sample</u>

The majority of the study respondents (53.6% or 5,598 students) were in school within the Baja California municipality of MexiCali. Tijiuana students represented the next largest proportion of the study sample (38.4%), followed by the much smaller municipalities of Tecate (6.5%) and Ensenada (1.4%). Of these students, 71.3% (N=7,444) were born and raised within the state of Baja California. Only 4.0% (N=418) of the sample was born outside of Mexico altogether. Given that the Culture of Lawfulness program is offered to ninth grade students, it is not surprising that a large majority of the sample (63.2%) were 14 years old; however, the ages did range from 13 years (14.5%) to include a small minority (15%) of 15 and 16 year olds. Slightly over half (51.2%) of the students were female.

Prior to participating in the Culture of Lawfulness program, ninety percent (90.1; N=9,371) of the students reported that they were "somewhat" to "very satisfied" with school; in contrast, 1,034 of the students reported some level of dissatisfaction with their school experience. Twenty eight percent (28.1%; N=2,930) of the sample responded that they were very good[8] students. The majority (52.6%; N=5,490) claimed they had an average grade ranking of 8, leaving 1,954 students (18.7%) with below average grades at the time of the current study.

Of particular interest given the research objectives of the current study, 1,833 students (17.6%) felt that they were likely to get involved in trouble in the future. Although most of the students reported non-involvement in delinquent activities over the previous sixty days, the sample did have some students that were engaged in serious activities. A large number of students (3,4671; 33.2%) had been involved in at least one fight in the last two months, with 983 (9.4%) engaged in three or more. Extending beyond the level of the school ground fights common to many adolescents, 1,562 (15.0%) of the sample claimed that they had attacked someone in the last month with the intent to seriously injure or even kill. Over four hundred youths (N=421) reported that they had been involved in such aggravated assaults three or more times in the last two months.

In terms of respecting the property of others, 2,902 (27.8%) of the respondents reported having intentionally broken or destroyed another person's property in the previous sixty days. As with the acts of physical violence, a smaller group within the sample (867 respondents) noted chronic acts of property damage of three or more incidents. Similarly, 9.1% (N=947) of the sample stole something of significant value at least once during the two months prior to instrument administration. Even more serious, almost nine hundred students (N=891; 8.5%) used physical force at least once to obtain money or another person's belongings.

The above patterns of delinquent activity also extended to the peer group the sample chose to be involved within in the last sixty days. Although 68.1% of the youths claimed that none of their friends had suggested they do something that is against the law, the remaining 3,103 youths (29.7%) had at least "a few" friends that did. Of these, 1,400 youths (13.4%) reported that "most" or "all" of their friends tried to influence them to break the law in some way. Thirty-four percent

---

[8] With a grade ranking of 9 or 10.

(34.3%) of the sample had at least some friends that were involved in gangs, with 1,233 (11.8%) reporting that most or all of their friends were gang members. While 66.7% of the sample did not have friends that had broken or destroyed another's property in the previous sixty days, this leaves 3,303 (31.6%) who did.

Prior to discussing the results, it is also important to examine the distribution of legal reasoning scores in the sample. Figure-4 offers a bar graph of respondent legal reasoning.

Figure 4 Distribution of Legal Reasoning Scores

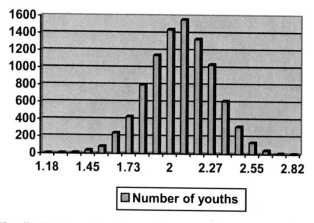

The distribution of legal reasoning scores is as would be expected based upon a review of the empirical literature discussed throughout the first three chapters of this work. Although not erasing all of the validity and reliability concerns for the legal reasoning measure offered in chapter five, the distribution allows us to be at least a little more confident in our results. The legal reasoning scores range from a low of 1.18 to a high pf 2.82, with a mean score of 2.06. Recall that this is slightly higher than that reported for American and Russian youths in the same age range (Finckenauer, 1995), but still lower in the conventional stages of reasoning that is characteristic of adolescents.

Summary of Model Fit Indices Used in the Study

Amos 5.0 (Arbuckle and Wothke, 2003) was used to test the proposed conceptual model described in the previous chapter. In addition to numerous advantages to using the Amos software, Amos offers a significant number of fit indices to assess the adequacy of fit between the sample data and the proposed model. The chi-square goodness of fit test statistic is one of the most common general measures of overall fit between the sample covariance and fitted covariance matrices (Hoyle, 1995). In reality, chi-square can be viewed as a "badness of fit" index in that smaller values actually indicate better fit – a value of zero indicates a perfect fit (Ibid.). Due to the sensitivity of this test to large sample sizes and its reliance on the assumptions of the central chi-square distribution,[9] many researchers have turned to alternative fit indices to assess model fit.

Most of the alternate fit indices really are "goodness of fit" measures, with higher scores indicating a greater fit between the observed and proposed models. These indices range in possible values from 0 to 1.0, with the latter indicating a perfect fit. Values of .95 and above are generally viewed as indicators of optimal fit with these indices (Hu and Bentler, 1995). Comparing the model to a baseline model (or independence model) will be the incremental fit indices, known as the comparative fit index (CFI) and the normed fit index (NFI). Finally, as a measure of the amount of error in the approximation of the population, the root mean square error of approximation index (RMSEA) will also be used. Unlike the previous fit indices, values of the RMSEA less than .05 indicate good fit; values ranging from .08 to .10 represent mediocre fit, and higher than .10 poor fit (Byrne, 1998). Some researchers have argued that the RMSEA always be used when a study only use maximum likelihood estimation – as most recent work now does given suggested problems with generalized least squares estimation (Sugawara and MacCallum, 1993).

---

[9] Assumption that the model fits perfectly in the population as per the null hypothesis (Byrne, 1998).

<u>Testing the Measurement Model: Confirmatory Factor Analysis (CFA)</u>

Confirmatory factor analysis tests the validity of an instrument by examining the degree to which items designed to measure a particular latent construct actually do so, and do not significantly load on other constructs. As a technique, it is generally considered most appropriate when "applied to measures that have been fully developed and their factor structures validated" (Byrne, pg.99). To a certain extent this requirement is met with the study instrument in that all of its scales were derived from pre-existing, validated measures. However, because some of the scale items had been removed at the discretion of the NSIC personnel many of the scales require revalidation. Additionally, none of the selected scales were previously validated in Spanish or with Mexican youth populations. Prior to the CFA, items that loaded too heavily with other constructs were either removed from the study, or if appropriate, added to the latent construct to which they empirically belonged (see chapter five for more detail on the EFA process). As illustrated in Figure-5, the proposed model for the CFA hypothesizes that the Mexican Culture of Lawfulness instrument can be explained by nine correlated latent constructs (factors) in which each indicator has a nonzero factor loading on the construct it was designed to measure, and zero loadings on all other factors (Byrne, 1998). The measurement error terms are also uncorrelated.

Model Assessment

The sample covariance matrix includes a total of 902 pieces of information or sample moments. Of the 279 parameters in the model, 169 are freely estimated and all other parameters are fixed. The model is overidentified with 733 degrees of freedom. With the exception of the χ^2 (733, N=10,436)=5076.98, p=.001, the fit indices showed that the sample data demonstrated a good fit with the proposed CFA model. Recall that smaller values of the chi-square are preferable but that it is also fairly susceptible to the influence of large sample sizes. The values for the CFI, NFI, and RMSEA were .93, .91, and .02 respectively. The confidence interval for the RMSEA was (.023 to .024).

Figure 5 Hypothesized 42-item model of the Factorial Structure for the Mexican Culture of Lawfulness Inventory

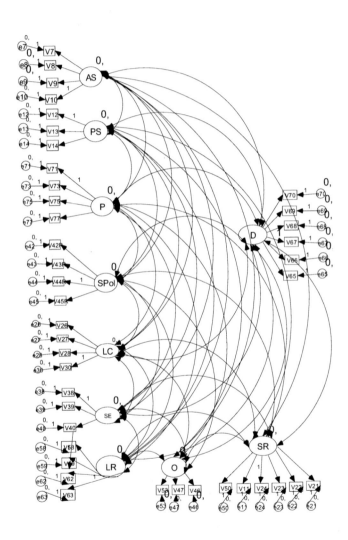

Given the relative confidence these indicators of fit give us in the fact that the study's latent constructs are loading together and not significantly with other constructs, no additional post-hoc analyses were necessary. It is important that these findings do not conclusively speak to the overall validity of the instrument scales. Additional testing of the instrument will be necessary to determine whether or not each scale is truly measuring what it is intended to measure. Remember that for some of the scales (i.e. self-esteem, legal reasoning) the overall internal consistency was less than desirable. We will return to this issue in the next chapter.

Table-7 presents the unstandardized and standardized regression weights for each of the nine latent variables of the current study. As noted in chapter five, some researchers use the criteria that each factor has a minimum loading of .30 on the latent construct it is intended to measure.[10] This standard was met for the majority of scale indicators. Not surprisingly given the results of the internal consistency, self-esteem, obligation, and legal reasoning fared the worst on this test.

Table 7 Regression Weights for the nine latent variables

VARIABLE	INDICATORS	FACTOR LOADINGS	
		Unstandardized	Standardized
Personal Safety	V14	1.70	.70
	V13	1.92	.83
	V12	1.00	.51
Peers	V77	1.17	.63
	V75	1.14	.65
	V73	1.08	.65
	V71	1.00	.55
Attitudes Toward School	V9	.76	.32
	V8	.67	.34
	V7	.88	.36
	V10	1.00	.53
Support for the Police	V45R	.85	.59
	V44R	1.00	.61
	V43R	.22	.42

[10] Standardized regression weights presented in bold highlight those items with a factor loading below of .30 on their desired construct.

VARIABLE	INDICATORS	FACTOR LOADINGS	
		Unstandardized	Standardized
	V42R	1.00	.60
Locus of Control	V30	1.00	.54
	V28	1.55	.79
	V27	1.07	.62
	V26	1.32	.67
Self-esteem	V40	7.48	.82
	V39	1.98	**.20**
	V38	1.00	**.12**
Legal Reasoning	V63	1.00	.33
	V62	1.04	.32
	V59	.76	**.28**
	V58	.58	**.20**
Obligation	V53	.51	**.29**
	V50	-.08	**-.04**
	V47	1.00	.62
	V46	.95	.53
Social Responsibility	V11	.88	.36
	V24	1.20	.54
	V23	1.00	.43
	V22	.84	.36
	V21	.71	**.29**
	V50	.98	.42
Delinquency	V70	.77	.55
	V69	1.00	.57
	V68	1.24	.59
	V67	1.00	.66
	V66	.78	.59
	V65	1.24	.61

The Proposed Baseline Model

The proposed model to be tested hypothesized the legal reasoning construct as a "full mediator" between perceptions of law enforcement, five other risk factors, social responsibility and obligation, and ultimately delinquency. Overall, the full mediation model had a very mediocre fit to the sample data χ^2 (753, N=10,436) = 8758.32, p = .001. The alternate fit indices were not much better, with a CFI of .86, NFI of .85, and RMSEA of .032 (confidence interval equals= .031 to .032).

The Revised Baseline Model

Structural equation modeling (SEM) allows for the re-specification of models in post-hoc analyses, assuming there is both a statistical and theoretical basis for doing so (Byrne, 1998). In conducting the post-hoc analyses, the researcher sought to examine the "mediation effect" of legal reasoning through a series of tests involving increasing the parameters of the original model to include a direct effect of each study variable on delinquency in addition to the pathway through legal reasoning (one at a time). This technique of mediation analyses (and those that follow below) can be accredited to the work of David Kenny (see Baron and Kenny, 1986). Squared multiple correlations were also examined each time for change in the amount of variance the model explained in the endogenous variables (i.e. legal reasoning, social responsibility, obligation, and delinquency).

In the course of doing this, three of the revised models failed to converge, indicating that there was a significant problem. Simply adding parameters should only enhance a model's fit rather than cause significant problems with convergence. In a final analysis, a direct effect of legal reasoning on delinquency was also tested, demonstrating significant positive changes in terms of the overall fit of the model, as will be detailed below. This suggested that a major part of the specification problem was in forcing all of the model's causal associations through legal reasoning, and in turn obligation/social responsibility, to ultimately impact upon delinquency. This is supported by the fact that re-running all of the prior mediation tests,[11] while at the same time allowing for a direct effect between legal reasoning and delinquency eliminated the problem evidenced with three of the prior runs.

Figure 6 Revised Hypothesized Model of the Effects of Support for the Police, Risk Factors and Legal Reasoning on Delinquency

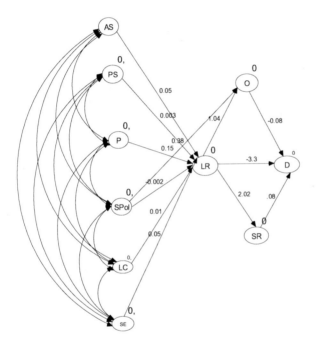

Figure-6 presents this revised baseline model, including the unstandardized regression weights. There are five endogenous variables

---

[11] Allowing direct effects for each of the exogenous variables one at a time, in addition to the "full mediation" through legal reasoning.

in this model (legal reasoning [LR], obligation [O], social responsibility [SR], and delinquency [D]). The exogenous variables proposed to impact upon each of these variables are attitudes toward school (AS), personal safety (PS), support for the police (SPol), locus of control (LC), and self-esteem (SE). There are 260 parameters in the model, of which 150 are to be freely estimated. The model is overidentified with 752 degrees of freedom.

Assessment of goodness of fit

Once again, given the sensitivity of the χ^2 to the extraordinarily large sample size of this sample, it is found to be a statistically significant statistic - χ^2 (752; N=10,437) = 6213.10, _p_ =.001. As a result it is necessary to turn to alternative fit indices. The CFI and NFI are .91 and .90 respectively for the revised model, indicating a good though not optimal overall fit; recall that researchers commonly refer to a .95 or above index as representing optimal fit (Byrne, 1998). The RMSEA, however, was well within the range of acceptability with a value of.026 (confidence interval=.026 to .027).

Review of parameter estimates

In the revised baseline model, legal reasoning was shown to have a much stronger direct effect on delinquency than originally hypothesized. For every one point advance in legal reasoning, delinquency decreases 3.30 points (-.84 standardized estimate). However, in support of the original hypotheses, legal reasoning also has a significant positive impact on both social responsibility (2.02 unstandardized; .44 standardized) and obligation (1.04 unstandardized; .18 standardized).

Also in support of the original model, obligation has a negative effect (-.08 unstandardized; -.11 standardized) on delinquency. However, these parameter estimates are far below their originally proposed importance. Although in the original model social responsibility had a very significant negative effect on delinquency (-1.20 unstandardized; -.73 standardized), when the direct effect from legal reasoning to delinquency was allowed in the revised model, this relationship disappeared to a slightly positive influence (.08 unstandardized; .09 standardized) on delinquency. All of its power on delinquency was thus being falsely forced through the path of legal reasoning.

Each of the exogenous variables had a statistically significant effect on legal reasoning (p<.001); however, only peers and attitudes towards school had a relationship worth noting. For every one point advance in the direction of positive peers, legal reasoning increases by .15 (.80 standardized). Attitudes toward school had the next largest impact on legal reasoning (.05 unstandardized; .20 standardized). Interestingly, support for the police had a slightly negative impact on legal reasoning (-.02 unstandardized;.-.10 standardized) contrary to expectations. We will return to the implications of this, and all of the above findings in the final chapter of the study.

Squared Multiple Correlations

In addition to a review of the overall fit indices, the squared multiple correlations allow for an additional understanding of the theoretical importance of a proposed model. Squared multiple correlations provide an assessment of the amount of variance for each endogenous variable that can be explained by the model's predictors. In this case, strong support is offered for the revised baseline model. Importantly it was estimated that the predictors of legal reasoning included in the model explain 85% of its variance. As the model ultimately rests on the explanatory power for delinquency, its squared multiple correlation is of critical importance: an R^2 of .69 estimates that 69% of the variance in delinquency can be explained by the model; such a large value for R^2 offers strong support for the predictive power of the revised baseline model. The remaining endogenous variables of obligation and social responsibility had R^2 values of .19 and .20 respectively.

Additional Post-hoc Analyses: the Power of Mediation with Direct Effects Added

After settling on the revised baseline model, additional post-hoc analyses were conducted to assess the overall power of legal reasoning as a mediating variable for each of the originally proposed exogenous variables (attitudes toward school, personal safety, peers, support for the police, locus of control and self-esteem). The results of these chi square difference tests are presented in Table-8. The table also includes changes in the R^2 values for each of the revised path models to include the additional direct effects.

Overall, adding the direct effects, in combination with a continued partial mediation of effects through legal reasoning, did not substantially change the overall fit of the model, or the parameters. This is important because another measure of model misspecification is the degree to which parameters bounce around with the addition or removal of parameters. Examination of changes in the R^2 values with modification to the model is also useful in assessing the degree to which changes in the χ^2 are simply a statistical artifact rather than meaningful change.

Not surprisingly, the χ^2 values did change somewhat with the addition of direct effects, particularly with respect to the relationship between peers and delinquency ($\chi^2_{diff} = 423.11$). However, even though this is the most notable change for models with a significant direct effect added, the overall fit indices remain virtually the same. Also interesting, the R^2_{diff} values for both legal reasoning and delinquency decrease fairly significantly (-.14 and -.08 respectively). In no case did an added direct effect increase the amount of delinquency's variance explained by the predictors more than two percent (2.0%). In fact, although the greatest χ^2 changes occurred in a model that included direct effects from all exogenous variables simultaneously ($\chi^2_{diff} = 532.75$), even here the R^2 values for both legal reasoning and delinquency decreased from the revised baseline model described above.

Table 8 Chi-square Difference Tests for the inclusion of Direct Effects from each Exogenous Variable

Effect	Regression co-efficient (standardized)	χ^2	χ^2 Difference[12]	Fit indices (CFI; RMSEA)	R^2 (LR; Del)	R^2 Difference[13]
Revised baseline model	------	6213.10	------	.91; .03	.85; .69	------
AS→Del.	.47 (.43)	6141.92 df=751 p<.001	71.18 p<.001	.91; .03	.92; .69	.07; 0
PS→Del.	.11 (.17)	6168.25 df=751 p<.001	44.85 p<.001	.91; .03	.86; .71	.01; .02
P→Del.	-.50 (-.67)	5718.81 df=751 p<.001	423.11 p<.001	.92; .03	.71; .61	-.14; -.08
SPol→Del	-.23 (.35)	6054.95 df=751 p<.000	86.97 p<.001	.91; .03	..85; 71	0; .02
LC→Del.	.23 (.40)	6010.82 df=751 p<.001	131.10 p<.001	.91; .03	.83; .77	-.02; .08
SE→Del.	.68 (.28)	6173.05 df=751 p<.001	40.05 p<.001	.91; .03	..87; .72	.02; .03
All→Del.	AS=.12 (.45) PS=.01 (.04) P =-.40 (.37) SPol=.-.12 (-.18) LC=.08 (.13) SE=.06 (.02)	5680.35 df=746 p<.001	532.75 p<.001	.92; .03	.75; .67	-.10; -.02

All of the preceding evidence seems to offer some preliminary support that the full mediation model for legal reasoning (allowing for a

---

[12] This column provides the difference in χ^2 value between the revised baseline model, and a new model with the direct effects added in column one.
[13] This column provides the difference in R^2 value between the revised baseline model, and a new model with the direct effects added in column one.

direct effect between legal reasoning and delinquency) may in fact have some validity. However, Table-8 also offers some cautionary findings before quickly accepting this conclusion. In all cases, the standardized regression co-efficients for the direct effects between the exogenous variables are not insignificant. Although this was to be expected given that each variable was drawn from substantial empirical support in the research literature, further analysis needed to be conducted in order to truly understand the nature and power of the legal reasoning mediating relationship or "insulation" from delinquency.

Additional Post-hoc Analyses: Removing the Mediation (or indirect) Effects

In this set of analyses, the mediation effect with legal reasoning was taken out one-by-one for each exogenous variable, allowing only for a direct effect between each variable and delinquency. These results are presented in Table-9. Similar to what was found when direct effects were added; taking out the legal reasoning mediation parameter entirely did not substantially affect the fit indices. The χ^2_{diff} values are all statistically significant; however, this is more likely the result of sample size than a factor worth emphasizing too much. Of the exogenous variables, peers again stood out as the strongest in terms of χ^2_{diff} when mediation was removed. However, as before, this was accompanied by a decrease in the explanatory power of the predictor variables on both legal reasoning and delinquency evidenced in their R^2 values.

What is most striking is the fact that the largest χ^2_{diff} value occurs in the final analysis: allowing all exogenous variables to simultaneously have a direct effect on delinquency, but with no mediation. Further support for the partial mediation model is that the χ^2 changed significantly towards poorer fit when mediation was completely removed from the model (from 6213.10 to 6896.09). Despite including more direct effects from variables known to exhibit strong influences on delinquency from the empirical literature, this model explains less of the variance in delinquency than in the revised baseline model.

Finally, comparing the direct effect regression coefficients in a model without any mediation (and only direct effects from all of the exogenous variables simultaneously) also suggests an important role of mediation in the causal structure of these variables. With the exception of peers, the regression coefficients between each exogenous variable and delinquency dropped. Legal reasoning appears to playing an important role in explaining the relationship between the exogenous variables and delinquency, even if it is not the "total mediation" model originally hypothesized. Based on the above results, the partial mediation model for legal reasoning and delinquency was selected as the final model of this study.

Table 9 Chi-square Difference Tests for the Inclusion of Direct Effects from each Exogenous Variable (eliminating mediation through legal reasoning)

Effect (no LR mediation)	Regression co-efficient (standardized) -with mediation	Regression co-efficient (standardized) - no mediation	χ^2	χ^2 Difference[14]	Fit indices CFI; RMSEA	R^2 (LR; Del)	R^2 Difference[15]
Revised baseline model	------	------	6213.10	------	.91; .03	.85; .69	------
AS→Del.	.47 (.43)	-.07 (-.07)	6280.25 df=752 p<.001	67.15 p<.001	.91; .03	.81; .71	-.04; .02
PS→Del.	.11 (.17)	.02 (.03)	6209.01 df=752 p<.001	4.09 p<.001	.91; .03	.86; .69	.01; .00
P→Del.	-.50 (-.67)	-.53 (-.02)	5912.41 df=752 p<.001	296.60 p<.001	.91; .03	.76; .61	-.09; -.08
SPol→Del.	-.23 (.35)	-.02 (-.02)	6244.57 df=752 p<.001	31.47 p<.001	.91; .03	.80; .74	-.05; .05
LC→Del.	.23 (.40)	.01 (.01)	6253.45 df=752 p<.001	40.35 p<.001	.91; .03	.85; .70	.00; .01

[14] This column provides the difference in χ^2 value between the revised baseline model, and a new model removing the indirect effects on delinquency between legal reasoning and each of the exogenous variables in column one.

[15] This column provides the difference in R^2 value for legal reasoning and delinquency between the revised baseline model, and a new model in which there is no indirect effect between legal reasoning and delinquency for the exogenous variable noted in column one.

Effect (no LR mediation)	Regression co-efficient (standardized) -with mediation	Regression co-efficient (standardized) - no mediation	χ^2	χ^2 Difference[14]	Fit indices CFI; RMSEA	R^2 [LR; Del]	R^2 Difference[15]
SE→Del.	.68 (.28)	-.04 (-.01)	6229.77 df=752 p<.001	16.67 p<.001	.91; .03	.86; .69	.01; .00
All→Del.	AS=.12 (.45) PS=.01 (.04) P =-.40 (.37) SPol=-.12 (-.18) LC=.08 (.13) SE=.06 (.02)	AS=-.09 (-.09) PS=-.00 (-.06) P =-.53 (-.71) SPol=.01 (.38) LC=-.00 (-.00) SE=-.09 (-.03)	6896.09 df=752 p<.001	615.84 p<.001	.89; .03	.00[16]; .61	-.85; -.08

<u>Fostering a Culture of Lawfulness: the partial mediation model of legal reasoning and delinquency</u>

Figure-7 presents the partial mediation model of legal reasoning and delinquency. To summarize, each of the selected exogenous variables [attitudes toward school (AS), personal safety (PS), support for the police (SPol), locus of control (LC), and self-esteem (SE)] have their own direct effect on delinquency. However, in addition, the model allows a portion of their causal power to continue to flow through the "partial mediator" of legal reasoning. This model continues to test the full mediation of legal reasoning of the effects of the exogenous variables on obligation and social responsibility.[17] The only variable given a direct effect on obligation aside from legal reasoning was support for the police, given the strength of this direct relationship in other work (Tyler, 1990), as reported in chapter two. The final model was overidentified with 746 degrees of freedom.

---

[16] The R^2 value for legal reasoning drops to .00 in this model because all predictor variables on legal reasoning have been removed.

[17] Thus, future research should reexamine the full mediation power of selected exogenous variables on obligation and social responsibility, as will be discussed in the next chapter.

Assessment of goodness of fit

Selecting this model evidences some gains in the χ^2 index of overall model fit compared to the revised baseline model presented above (χ^2_{diff} = 532.75; p<.001). The χ^2 (746, N=10,436) value for the final model is 5680.35 (p=.001)[18]. The fit indices for the CFI, NFI, and RMSEA are .92, .91, and .025. The confidence interval for the RMSEA is .025 to .026. This also represents a slightly better fit than the "pure mediation" model.

---

[18] Recall that the χ^2 value for the revised baseline model (full mediation of exogenous variables on delinquency through legal reasoning, obligation, and social responsibility) was 6215.10.

Figure 7 Final Study Model - Partial Mediation Effect of Legal Reasoning on Delinquency

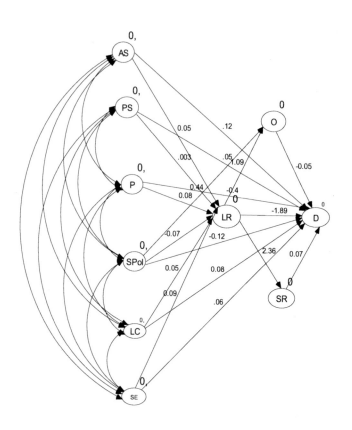

Changes to the parameter estimates

Given the large sample size, a criterion for the substantive effects of the exogenous variables on legal reasoning cannot rely solely on statistical significance, as this will largely be driven by the number of respondents in the sample. Instead, in examining each of the regression coefficients for exogenous variables on legal reasoning, a determination must be made as to their "substantive" importance. For example, in the final model, personal safety was the only variable that proved to have a statistically insignificant relationship effect on the level of legal reasoning ($p < .09$).

For this study, "substantive importance" was determined based upon an ability of each predictor to raise legal reasoning by at least .5. Recall that the legal reasoning score exists on a continuum between 1 and 3; scores above the "halfway point" (i.e. 1.5; 2.5) are considered to be "stage transitional", facilitating movement towards the next higher level of reasoning. As each level encompasses two stages (see chapter two), an increase of .5 is the equivalent of one advancing one stage in reasoning. If, given the size of a predictor's unstandardized regression co-efficient and the range of possible scores for that variable (i.e. 1-4; 1-5, etc.), legal reasoning can be advanced towards a "transitional" stage, its effects on legal reasoning are determined to be "substantively", as well as "statistically" significant.

In the final model, attitudes toward school has the most influence on legal reasoning (.14 unstandardized; .45 standardized), followed by self-esteem (.09 unstandardized; .12 standardized), peers (.08 unstandardized; .37 standardized), a still negative support for the police (-.07 unstandardized; -.38 standardized), and locus of control (.08 unstandardized; .30 standardized). Based on the above criterion, each of these predictors is having an important enhancing effect on legal reasoning. Attitudes towards school is a four item scale; therefore, it has the potential to increase legal reasoning level by .6. Having positive peers is represented on a seven point scale, thus having the "power" to increase legal reasoning one stage (.6). On the other hand, self-esteem exists on a three point scale and thus only has the capacity to raise legal reasoning level by .3, below our criteria for substantive importance. Similarly, locus of control (although in the right direction), can only increase legal reasoning by .2 of a level. Finally, support for the police has a retarding effect on legal reasoning (-.07), but this amounts to only the equivalent of .3 of a level, below our criterion of importance. However, the fact that increased support for the police has a negative effect on legal reasoning is contrary to our hypothesis and its theoretical meaning will be re-examined in chapter seven.

Legal reasoning continues to exhibit a strong influence on both obligation (1.09 unstandardized; .21 standardized) and social responsibility (2.36 unstandardized; .57 standardized). In all the revised models, a direct effect was allowed between support for the police and obligation given the strong connection between these variables noted in numerous studies (Tyler, 1990). Interestingly, in the final model, legal reasoning has a stronger regression coefficient for obligation than support for the police. For every one point increase in legal reasoning, obligation to obey the law also increases by 1.09 points (.21 standardized). This is compared to a coefficient of .44 (.45 standardized) for support for the police.

Obligation (-.05 unstandardized; -.07 standardized) and social responsibility (.07 unstandardized; .08 standardized) continue to have a statistically significant effect on delinquency, although it is clear that most of their original impact on self-reported behavior was due to the effects being "forced" through the mediating legal reasoning variable. The slightly positive association of social responsibility with delinquency will need further attention in the discussion.

Significantly, even allowing for the direct effects of each of the exogenous variables on delinquency, legal reasoning (-1.89 unstandardized; -.53 standardized) and peers (-.40 unstandardized; -.53 standardized) continue to have the most significant effects on delinquency. As noted in the mediation analysis, greater support for the police also has a significantly negative effect on delinquency, decreasing it .115 (-.18 standardized) for every one point increase in its own scale. An internal locus of control has a positive association with delinquency as hypothesized (.08 unstandardized; .13 standardized). Contrary to our hypotheses, higher self esteem is slighted associated (.06 unstandardized; .02 standardized) with an increase in delinquency. A perception of personal safety was the only variable that did not have a significant causal effect on the level of self-reported delinquency in the final model. The final model continues to include personal safety even though it did not exhibit a statistically significant causal effect on either legal reasoning or delinquency given its central importance to the overall study hypotheses; future research will thus need to re-examine this issue with possibly more concrete measures (i.e. recorded crime, gang activity, etc.) of risk factors from within the community domain. A deeper analysis of the theoretical and practical importance of these findings will be returned to in the final chapter.

Squared multiple correlations

The amount of variance in legal reasoning and delinquency explained in the model, decreased slightly from the revised baseline model; however, the balance of factors discussed above explain why the researcher has identified the "partial mediation" model as offering the best fit to the sample data, as well as theoretical and practical importance. The R^2 value for legal reasoning decreased from .85 to .75; the R^2 value for delinquency declined only slightly (from .69 to .67).

Summary

Following a series of post-hoc analyses, the "full mediation" model of legal reasoning was rejected. This was first initiated with the realization that there was a better fit of the sample data to a model which allowed a direct effect between legal reasoning and delinquency. Although legal reasoning had a significant effect on both of the attitudinal mediating variables (i.e. obligation and social responsibility), it had a stronger effect on delinquency on its own.

A series of mediation analyses revealed that, not surprisingly, each of the study exogenous variables had their own, not insignificant, effect on delinquency. However, additional analyses also demonstrated that the sample data exhibited a better overall fit to a model that included a "partial mediator" in legal reasoning; that is, each variable had its own direct effect on delinquency in addition to a path through legal reasoning. Legal reasoning and peer associations stand out as the variables with the most significant association with self-reported delinquency.

Also interesting, support for the police actually retarded legal reasoning to some degree, but also continued to exhibit a negative effect on delinquency. More belief in the fairness of law enforcement is associated with less delinquent acts, at the same time as it is linked to lower levels of legal reasoning.

CHAPTER SEVEN

Discussion

Mexico solidario acabo a los tiranos
Sin la necesidad de ensuciarnos las manos
No podemos pedir resultado inmediato
De un legado de setentacinco anos
Todos unidos pedimos un cambio
Pierda sobre pierda y peldano a peldano
Solo poder expresarnos
Es palabra de honor de nuestro jefe de estado.
Te arrepentiras de todo lo que trabajas
Se te ira la mitad de todo lo que tu ganas
Manteniendo los puestos de copias piratas
Que no pagan impuestos pero son mas baratas
Veo una fuerte campana de tele y radio
Promoviendo la union entre los ciudadanos
Mensaje de un pueblo libre y soberando
Igual que tu Molotov tambien es mexicano.
Molotov – Hit Me (Gimme tha Power II).

<u>Introduction</u>

The above words from a popular Mexican group summarize the frustrations and hopes for change in the minds of young Mexicans, speaking of a time without tyranny, pushing for a united citizenry, but at the same time recognizing that such a change cannot happen overnight after a legacy of seventy-five years.

The causal pathway between legal culture, risk factors, legal reasoning, and behavior proved to be more complex than originally hypothesized, although study results are consistent in many ways with expectations. For the most part, the selected risk factors did influence the strength of legal reasoning (both in terms of its level and effect on delinquency). Support for the police surprisingly had a retarding effect on legal reasoning.

Legal reasoning also exhibited a stronger relationship with delinquency than described in the study hypotheses. Rather than being mediated through the attitudes of obligation to obey the law (legitimacy factor 2) and social responsibility, it was shown that legal reasoning played a stronger direct role on delinquency, whether the direct effects of predictors were included in the model or not.

Finally, the power of legal reasoning as an "insulator" against the known criminogenic effects of selected risk factors was examined. Although the full mediation model was not supported, evidence for a better fit of a partial mediation model to the data (as opposed to allowing all exogenous variables to directly effect delinquency without mediation) was provided.

In this final chapter, the implications of all of these findings will be discussed, both in terms of criminological theory and criminal justice programming. Suggestions for future research and instrument development will also be offered.

Connections Between Legal Culture and Behavior

The primary research hypotheses focused on the important relationship between legal context (macro level) and individual likelihood to engage in delinquent activities (micro level). Given the importance placed by legal socialization theory on role-taking opportunities and the observation of fair processes for the creation and application of the laws, a measure was sought to examine the relationship between legal culture, legal reasoning, and behavior. As this study utilized cross-sectional data, and did not involve a comparison across more global legal contexts, a proxy variable of perceptions of law enforcement fairness was selected to be a measure of legal culture. As theory suggests that stimulating an appreciation of the need for laws and a moral conviction in the same will be influenced by legitimate enforcement practices, it was thought that perceptions of law enforcement fairness would have a significant effect on legal reasoning. It did have an effect on legal reasoning, just in the opposite direction to what was expected.

In hindsight this finding that perceptions of law enforcement fairness may actually retard legal reasoning actually makes perfect sense. Particularly in a legal context such as Mexico, where fair enforcement of the law is not the norm, too much belief in the fairness of the police might represent a cognitive naiveté characteristic of level one or level two thinking rather than postconventional thought. Recall that on these lower levels, blind obedience to the law is a significant possibility, either out of a fear of punishment and all authority figures, or an uncritical acceptance of the need for strict enforcement of rules and laws in society, regardless of their moral validity. This supposition of possible naiveté is supported in the post-test data of the Mexican youths included in the current study. As described in chapter four, the evaluation found that those youths who had participated in the 60 lesson Culture of Lawfulness program actually believed less in the fairness of police at the end of the course. Importantly, they were significantly more likely to respond that they would support the police more if they enforced the law more in accordance with the rule of law.

However, belief in the fairness of law enforcement did have an important direct negative effect on delinquency, supporting previous studies on the connection between attitudes towards the police and delinquency discussed in chapter two. This finding also supports the hypothesis that there is a connection between legal culture and behavior; it is just that the connection with legal reasoning is itself more complicated than anticipated. The post-hoc mediation analyses revealed that the negative effect of the support for the police variable on delinquency was actually higher through the partial mediator of legal reasoning than on its own, providing further support for the original study hypotheses.

An important finding for the legal socialization literature is that legal reasoning has a very significant direct effect on delinquency, without having to be mediated through attitudinal mediators, as suggested by Cohn and White (1990). These findings actually support the work of Finckenauer (1995) more strongly. Even allowing for each of the exogenous variables to have direct effects on delinquency without any mediation through legal reasoning, this cognitive variable continued to exhibit the strongest influence on delinquency (although understandably with decreased power) of all the predictor variables in the model (along with positive peer associations). These findings suggest support for the legal socialization model connecting fair enforcement with legal reasoning and ultimately behavior; however, it should also be noted that the direct effect of legal reasoning on delinquency in this model could be due to the inclusion of the wrong attitudinal mediators.

For example, the work of Cohn and White suggested that legal reasoning had a more complex relationship with behavior, being mediated through the attitudinal variables of normative status and enforcement status (see chapter two). Although this study also examined a similar path of attitudinal mediators between legal reasoning and delinquency, the attitudinal variables selected were not the same as those in the Cohn and White (1990) study. In this case, the two attitudinal variables selected for study were obligation to obey the law and social responsibility. Although these variables are very relevant to the legal socialization literature and the hypotheses of the current study, future research may want to replicate some of the SEM analyses from this study while including the Cohn and White (1990) measures of normative status and enforcement status described in chapter two.

It was hypothesized that increased legal reasoning would lead to an increased sense of obligation to obey the law in addition to greater levels of social responsibility. These variables were then each thought to influence delinquency directly. The first part of this model was supported, but not the latter. Legal reasoning did significantly increase both obligation to obey the law and social responsibility; however, while increased obligation is negatively associated with the frequency of self-reported delinquency, social responsibility actually evidenced a slight increase in delinquent behavior. As noted above, in this study the direct effect of legal reasoning on behavior is stronger than the indirect effect.

The inconsistency of these findings can likely be explained by the fact that a wealth of social psychological research has indicated that the relationship between attitudes and behavior are not always as consistent as we tend to think (Worden, 1995). Legal reasoning, on the other hand, is a cognitive measure of how one looks at rules and laws to organize information and resolve conflicts, rather than a specific attitudinal measure. In the end, this may have a stronger relationship on delinquency than simply attitudinal constructs. This suggests that legal reasoning plays an important role in generating positive attitudes towards the law and one's role in the community, but these attitudes themselves are not sufficient to determine whether or not one is likely to always choose to act on these beliefs. The attitudes might be more susceptible to situational factors than the cognitive construct of legal reasoning. Future research needs to examine this relationship further.

Tyler's (1990) study of the relationship between perceptions of the fairness of law enforcement and behavior found that a belief in the legitimacy of rules and laws (obligation) was related to overall the perceived fairness of law enforcement conduct. This, in turn, influenced one's likelihood to comply with the law. This relationship was supported with the current sample. In addition to a mediating effect with legal reasoning, a direct effect was allowed between support for the police and obligation given the strong relationships between these variables evidenced in the literature. Interestingly, while this path was significant in this model, the effect of legal reasoning on obligation was stronger than that of support for the police on its own, once again providing additional support for the importance of reasoning about rules and laws in understanding the relationship between perceptions, attitudes, and behavior.

As noted above, future studies need to test this model with more concrete, global measures of legal context than were within the scope of this study. A reliance on the perceptions of law enforcement fairness as a measure of legal context is too susceptible to other factors possibly unique to the individual respondent rather than the actual nature of law enforcement in an area. The possibilities of replicating this study in other countries implementing the Culture of Lawfulness program will likely provide a more meaningful understanding of law enforcement practice and corruption on legal socialization.

Effect of Risk Factors on Legal Reasoning

This study conceptualized legal reasoning as a possible mediating factor, insulating an individual from the known criminogenic influences of risk factors established in the criminological literature. Risk factors from all but one of the five risk factor domains were examined in this study: attachment to school (school), personal safety (community), self esteem and locus of control (individual), and delinquent peers (peers). Regrettably, the Mexican Culture of Lawfulness instrument did not include any measures of family-related factors. Each of these variables was hypothesized to have an either retarding or accelerating effect on legal reasoning in accordance with the resiliency literature. The current study tested the effects of the selected exogenous variables on delinquency only through an examination of the parameter estimates; the free parameters do not contribute to the testable fit of the model. Moreover, as detailed in the previous chapter, the researcher could not rely solely on a review of statistical significance in terms of assessing these effects – instead, it was determined that each predictor needed to have the potential to advance legal reasoning the equivalent of a stage (or .5 in value).

With the sole exception of personal safety, each of the selected risk factors exhibited the hypothesized effect on legal reasoning. The variables with the strongest effect on legal reasoning were positive peer associations and school attachment; both had a positive effect on the level of legal reasoning. These variables are particularly significant in that they most accurately represent the informal rule structures of society, in contrast to the formal legal culture of fair law enforcement. Finckenauer (1995) stressed that an overall assessment of both formal and informal rule enforcing contexts are important in understanding legal socialization. In this case, having peers that reinforce the importance of rules and positive values might provide some of the role-taking activities and stimulation necessary for legal reasoning advancement. Similarly, an attachment to school could lead to self-created opportunities for increased critical thinking and knowledge that can influence legal reasoning development according to the dictates of legal socialization theory.

The finding that an internal locus of control also leads to increases in legal reasoning is important for the overall culture of lawfulness approach. With an internal locus of control, individuals feel more in control of their own destiny regardless of context, and thus believe they can overcome obstacles to becoming who they want to be. Such an outlook is also logically associated with manipulating the environmental constraints so as to create role-taking opportunities for him or herself. In addition to increasing the likelihood of legal reasoning advancement possibilities, such a person might be more inclined to take action in his or her community, and not tolerate criminal or corrupt activities. The obvious sequence from locus of control to legal reasoning to social responsibility thus makes sense.

The fact that increased concern about personal safety did not have a significant effect on legal reasoning warrants further study. It may be that, like our measure for legal culture, perceptions of personal safety are not adequate or consistent enough to get a true sense of community level risk factors. Instead, future studies should combine such measures of perception with sounder measures of public safety such as recorded levels of crime, disorder, and gang activity.

Legal reasoning continued to have a large negative direct effect on delinquency even in the "no mediation model" (in which it did not include the "power" of the indirect causal effects of each of the predictor variables). However, the direct effect between legal reasoning and delinquency was, not surprisingly, strongest in the partial mediation model. Significantly, with our final selected model 75% of the variance in legal reasoning is accounted for by the predictors in the model. In turn, the model accounts for 67% of the variance in delinquency.

<u>Mediation Power of Legal Reasoning</u>

Although supporting evidence was not found for a complete mediation model of legal reasoning, post-hoc analyses did indicate that at least there were important partial mediation effects occurring. This makes sense given the known significant effects of each of the exogenous variables on delinquency prior to their selection for the model. The findings thus force us to take a more realistic, tempered view of the "insulating" power of legal reasoning on the negative effects of established risk factors. Legal reasoning may be able to offset some of the influences of risk factors, but only up to a point.

As noted above without allowing for partial mediation, the direct effects of each of the risk factor variables decrease significantly, whereas legal reasoning continues to have a strong effect on delinquency. An examination of the direct effects without any mediation presented some interesting patterns. In support of Baumeister (2001), without any mediation, self-esteem has a slightly positive effect on delinquency; thus supporting our claim that many of the established protective factors such as self-esteem or problem-solving are necessary, but by themselves may not be sufficient without a positive cognitive orientation towards rules, laws, and principals of justice. This is an area that definitely requires the attention of future research.

<u>Statistically Equivalent Models</u>

MacCallum, Wegener, Uchino & Fabrigar, (1993) argue that many researchers using SEM techniques fail to take into account alternative models that may fit their sample data. In fact, a good fit for one model implies that there would be a good fit for other equivalent models. Different models are equivalent if they have the same general pattern of partial correlations in them. The more complex a model is, the greater the number of possibilities for more equivalent models there are.

It is impossible to account for all alternative possibilities, but theory or previous research can rule out some of these important options. A major question with respect to both moral and legal reasoning is whether or not legal reasoning causes behavior, or vice versa. It has been suggested that legal reasoning might represent a form of cognitive restructuring to justify one's actions.

As the current study was a cross-sectional design, it is impossible to argue conclusively for the causal direction between legal reasoning and behavior. However, the Cohn and White study (1990) upon which much of the study hypotheses were based involved the measurement of university students on legal reasoning both at the beginning and end of the school year. Although they did not find a direct relationship between legal reasoning and behavior, compliance levels in the external authority condition were lower where legal reasoning also declined over the course of the year. They found that the enforcement condition influenced legal reasoning which then influenced the attitudinal mediators responsible for law compliance by the end of the spring semester.

The Cohn and White (1990) study thus also plausibly helps us to eliminate the possibility of legal reasoning impacting perceptions of law enforcement fairness rather than the other way around. The students in their study differed significantly in terms of legal reasoning levels by virtue of their participation in the external authority or peer authority enforcement conditions over the year. Similarly, much of the empirical findings by Tyler (1990; 2000) support the directional pathway between perceptions of law enforcement fairness, obligation, and law compliance. This research helps us to be more secure in our connections between our final model's directions between support for the police, legal reasoning, and social responsibility/obligation. However, once again, it is argued that the effect of more concrete global measures of legal context on legal reasoning should be compared across countries in future research.

It is possible that legal reasoning might lead to the level of attachment one feels to the school rule structures and the selection of peer groups that share his or her worldview. This possibility is more difficult to argue against in that there is no precedent for research that draws these direct conditions until this study. While these relationships clearly warrant further research that can better separate out the timing of the causal sequence, legal socialization in general would likely argue that the role-taking opportunities and critical thinking offered by peer selection and school attachment would more likely influence levels of legal reasoning than the reverse to be true.

Similarly, it is more theoretically plausible that one's locus of control might influence an individual to cognitively structure the world in terms of the strict needs for external constraints (levels one and two) or internalized controls (level three) than the other way around. However, as with the school attachment and selection of peer associations, these relationships are too untested to argue conclusively against.

To summarize, all of the above effects need to be interpreted with caution, and remain conditional based on the assumptions built into the model. Most importantly, future research needs to build on this effort with increased attention to strengthening the reliability and validity of some of this study's measures, particularly legal reasoning.

<u>Strength of the Legal Reasoning Measure</u>

This study of legal socialization is unprecedented in terms of the power gained by the size of its sample of Mexican youths. However, as highlighted throughout chapter five, a review of both the reliability and validity of its core measure – legal reasoning – are a cause for concern, and warrant caution in interpreting the above theoretically interesting and important findings. It should be stressed here, however, that despite the possible structural problems with the legal reasoning measure, its concurrent validity is mildly supported by the fact that it is sufficiently correlated with (and in the hypothesized directions) with virtually all of the other scales included in this study. Additionally, the distribution of respondent legal reasoning scores provided in chapter six is in alignment with what one would expect for a population of this age group based upon a review of the literature. That being said, future research needs to expend resources developing a sound empirical base for the measurement of legal reasoning, as has been the case with its moral reasoning predecessor.

The measurement of legal reasoning began with a series of open-ended questions which ask respondents to reflect on the nature, importance, and use of rules and laws in society (Tapp and Levine, 1977). Because they were open-ended, the researcher could capture the specific nuances of each individual's response and then code it accordingly as to the stages and/or levels of legal reasoning. The important work of Cohn and White (1990) discussed throughout this study used this instrument with its university sample. Thus, the original legal reasoning instrument is similar to Kohlberg's Moral Judgment Interview (MJI) measurement of moral reasoning in that it requires one-on-one interviews between the researcher and respondent, and numerous time to sift through and code each response.

However, from the outset, measurement of legal reasoning differed significantly from its MJI cousin in that the latter principally involved respondent review of moral dilemmas, and discerning how he or she might respond. Although clearly this does not replicate the nuances of a real-world situation, it paints a strong picture related to how an individual reasons through moral challenges. It is the opinion of this researcher, that the measurement of legal reasoning should involve similar situation-based scenarios, with a focus on the importance of rules and laws governing each situation. This would provide the researcher a more realistic appraisal of how an individual views rules and laws across situational contexts, and whether or not he or she is governed by a punishment orientation towards the law or otherwise in accordance with legal socialization theory.

There is some empirical literature to support these assertions, comparing the psychometric properties of production versus recognition measures of moral reasoning. Production measures, of which the MJI is the most notable example, involve respondent review of moral dilemmas upon which a series of moral judgments are to be made. The respondent is then asked to provide justifications for each of their determinations. Other commonly used production measures of moral reasoning include the Sociomoral Reflection Measure (Gibbs and Widaman, 1982) and the Sociomoral Reflection Measure Short Form (Gibbs, Basinger & Fuller, 1992).

Recognition measures, as their name suggests, involve close-ended multiple choice formats in which the respondents evaluate a list of statements and are asked to select the one which best matches their level of reasoning. Three recognition measures have been most commonly used for the measurement of moral reasoning: the Defining Issues Test (Rest, 1999), Sociomoral Reflection Reflection Objective Measure (Gibbs, Arnold, Ahlborn & Cheesman, 1984), and the Sociomoral Reflection Objective Measure-Short Form (Basinger and Gibbs, 1987). The 11 item legal reasoning scale used in the current study is the only existing recognition measure known to the researcher, and was previously utilized by Finckenauer (1995) and Jones Brown (1996).

Although the eleven questions currently in the scale can be used as a guideline for the creation of a revised instrument, it is the opinion of this researcher that the questions as they are currently are too abstract as to draw meaningful responses, particularly with a ninth grade study population. While an open-ended format may be able to overcome some of these difficulties by being able to capture specifically how the individual responds to each item, the close-ended format presents confining language that in many cases is difficult to understand. Add to this the problems with translation to another language and context, and it is believed that we have the reason for the instrument's low internal consistency. Only the four items included in the analysis are clear enough to be a useful measure of youth reasoning about rules and laws. Comparison studies of production and recognition measures of moral reasoning have found recognition measures to result in higher moral reasoning scores (Palmer, 2003) and to not be appropriate for use with younger respondents or people with reading or attention span problems (Gibbs, Arnold, Ahlborn & Cheesman, 1984). It is thus very possible that the reading comprehension level of the current study sample may have influenced their ability to adequately respond.

It should be stressed that the demands of conducting studies of large populations makes the original instrument impossible. Imagine interviewing 10,436 youths and then coding their responses! Thus, a revised close-ended instrument will be essential for future expansions of this exploratory study's findings. Although initially rejected by orthodox Kohlbergians, the Defining Issues Test (DIT) involves a close-ended recognition response format for the measurement of moral reasoning that allows for large sample study, at the same time as it retains the original measure's use of moral dilemmas to gauge respondent reasoning (Rest et al, 1999). This instrument has been continuously evaluated over the last thirty years and has produced a body of research that even the original open-ended format could not (i.e. the greater prevalence of postconventional thinking schemas in the population).

Although a complete review of this body of work is beyond the scope of this study, efforts to revise the legal reasoning instrument could draw upon its example. It should also be stressed that the recognition measures have made the measurement of moral reasoning more practical, without involving the extensive training and difficult coding practices common to the MJI and other production methods (Palmer, 2003).

With respect to developing a new measure of legal reasoning, once a draft instrument is created, focus groups should be held with relevant populations (e.g. youths, adults, police, lawyers, etc.) to generate different response categories (and possibly versions) of the instrument. With a revised instrument in hand based upon the focus group results, the long process of validation can begin. It is hoped that a balance can be found between the benefits of production measures of legal reasoning and the large-sample practicalities offered by recognition measures. As noted above, special attention will be provided to the use of scenarios that can more adequately stimulate respondent reasoning about the importance of rules and laws than the current abstract question format. As a word of caution, the artificiality of the situations involved in moral dilemmas has been found to be a problem for young children (Damon, 1977) and non –Western cultures (Boyes and Walker, 1988) by some researchers.

Practical Applications: Towards a Democratic Model of Policing and Criminal Justice

Despite some of the problems with instrumentation described above and in chapter four, this study produced some very interesting findings and preliminary support for many of the study hypotheses. The connection between legal culture and behavior was evident both in terms of the direct impact of perceptions of law enforcement on delinquency, and the strong relationship found between legal reasoning and delinquency. The important pathway between support for the police, obligation, and delinquency should also be highlighted.

Probably the most critical finding is legal reasoning's role as a partial mediator of the effects of such risk factors as locus of control, school attachment, self esteem, and peer associations. Although not a complete "silver bullet", legal reasoning appears to be playing an important role in ultimately determining whether or not given a balance of factors, an individual will engage in delinquent activity. In fact, this cognitive measure had a greater influence than the tested attitudinal measures of social responsibility and obligation to obey the law.

The final model provides preliminary support for the culture of lawfulness approach that forms the theoretical underpinnings of this work given its emphasis on legal culture (support for the police), legal reasoning, and behavior. The role of legal reasoning in the delinquency equations warrants future research on the types of curricula and other role-taking approaches that can successfully facilitate stage advancement. An increased research base in this area can, in turn, inform the Culture of Lawfulness curriculum, and related efforts around the world.

From the individual level, the fact that locus of control and attachment to school impact on legal reasoning suggests two important areas that should be addressed in crime prevention or law-related educational activities. Creating interactive curricula within the schools that offer students a chance to participate in rule creation and governance are just one example of how this might be achieved. Influencing a youth's locus of control might require techniques that inspire self-reflection and problem-solving skill development. The important role of peers as both facilitators and barriers to youthful law-abiding behavior has been stressed in the criminological literature for many years, and supported with this study's findings. Although a very difficult challenge to address in school-based or even rehabilitative programming with offending populations, innovative methods to challenge students to critically think about the positive and negative consequences of their associations need to be developed.

As illustrated in the Hong Kong and Palermo examples, even the best laid plans in the school will ultimately be futile if not combined with work in the other needed sectors of society. Even though this occurred in both of these contexts, teachers often expressed frustration with the "disqualifying power" of the world outside of the classroom (Schneider, 1998). Authors such as Bahn (1973) have long since argued about the perils of "counter training" in which the effects of training are nullified by counterforces in the workplace or larger society.

With respect to fostering a culture of lawfulness, it has been argued that society needs two primary forces: fair and effective law enforcement, and a culture in support of the rule of law (higher levels of postconventional thinking). The integral relationship between these two "wheels" has been the focus of study hypotheses. Similar efforts to the school-based education need to be taken into the other sectors of society for both training and reform. In the case of Mexico, such efforts are beginning in the area of police training. In addition to the need for an increased professional force with greater mechanisms for public accountability and scrutiny, many studies of police culture have emphasized the dangers of a "war on crime mentality" given its potential for leading to human rights violations. It may be the case (though there has been no research in this area) , that police are locked in the law and order orientation of level two reasoning, and that police training needs to try and facilitate movement towards level three principles of fairness and justice; the need for increased collaboration with the community should also be stressed.

Authors such as Barber (2000) have correctly argued that the transition of societies from totalitarian states to democracy represent the most dominant international challenges in the current century. An examination of the difficult progress in war-torn areas such as the Middle East, Afghanistan, and Iraq provide a host of ready examples. Promoting the rule of law along with the participation of a supportive civil society is not an easy venture in societies that are themselves overwhelmed with the problems of crime and corruption (Nield, 2001). In fact, as societies move away from the forced order of authoritarian rule, increased crime rates are often the unfortunate by-product. In response, law enforcement has often felt the need to become even more repressive in its attempts to restore order, and may even have the support of many segments (usually the middle and upper classes) of society (Chevigny, 1999). However, "in a democratic society, the dominant characteristic is the value placed on freedom" (Wiatrowski & Pitchard, pg. 8). However, it is a viscious circle because where society lives in fear of crime, greater value will be likely to be placed upon physical security than civil rights and liberties. So how then can a civil society emerge that is capable of advancing beyond the post-conflict crisis?

The important role of legal culture in stimulating civic participation has been the subject of this effort, and needs to be advanced further in later research. In order to be able to promote post-conventional thought in a civic society that is in support of the rule of law, there are several requirements of police and other societal organizations: (the following are modified from Wiatrowski, 2003):

- Accountability – organizations should be accountable to the society that creates them;
- Transparency – the institution is visible to the public that created it;
- Reflective of the rule of law – the principles of fairness and justice guide all police investigations and subsequent criminal justice responses;
- Legitimacy – as a product of all of the above, the majority of society will comply with the law out of willingness rather than coercion.

As noted by Wiatrowski (2003), "the police must recognize that the extent to which they violate these democratic requirements, they lose their legitimacy or the ability to demand voluntary compliance with legal orders" (pg.10). The failure of police organizations to recognize that their authority is derived from civil society is a key factor in contributing to crime and corruption (Ibid; Tyler, 1990). Thus, efforts at both law enforcement organizational reform and training need to try to get this message across to police agencies, even in societies where crime, corruption, and a corresponding "war on crime" model dominate.

It has been argued throughout this dissertation that by creating a legal culture that is grounded in democratic values and human rights, a sense of stakeholdership will begin to develop amongst civic society can function as informal norms and networks capable of counter-acting many of the criminogenic factors of societies and communities – it is for this reason that fostering a culture of lawfulness is not something that can occur overnight, but rather will take generations, as was the case in Palermo and Hong Kong. In line with this argument, Kelling and Coles (1996) have argued that trust networks can be rebuilt in communities where the police work with the community in norms enforcement rather than unilaterally enforcing their own standards and behavior.

In this sense, the theoretical and empirical literature that has been the subject of this literature can also be related to the social capital framework. Where communities begin to reduce disorder and overcome the formerly characteristic sense of helplessness that results from both offender and police impunity, norms such as reciprocity, civic engagement, social trust and collective action will emerge, that in time will add further support to the development and sustainability of a culture of lawfulness.

APPENDIX A

ENCUESTA PARA ESTUDIANTES

(Septiembre 2001)

Nos interesa conocer tu opinión sobre ti mismo, tu escuela y tus actividades. Te pedimos que respondas con sinceridad a las siguientes preguntas. Queremos conocer lo que los estudiantes en tu escuela piensan y hacen. No existen respuestas correctas o equivocadas. **Esto NO es un examen.** Lee cuidadosamente la pregunta y **TODAS** las respuestas antes de hacer tu elección.

No queremos tu nombre en la hoja de respuesta. Tus respuestas son **ANÓNIMAS**. Las respuestas de muchos estudiantes serán promediadas.

En la hoja de respuestas anexa donde dice
- NAME/NOMBRE, escribe el nombre de TU MAESTRO(A)
- DATE/FECHA, proporciona la FECHA de hoy
- PERIOD/GRUPO, escribe tu GRUPO.

Por favor marca tus respuestas en la hoja de respuestas anexa. Rellena completamente la burbuja correspondiente a tu respuesta. **NO** escribas tus respuestas en este cuestionario.

Por último, por favor no hables o compares respuestas con tus compañeros. Si en cualquier momento tienes alguna pregunta, levanta la mano.

¿QUIÉN ERES?

1. Eres:
   - o   Mujer
   - o   Hombre

2. ¿Cuántos años tienes?
   - o   13 años
   - o   14 años
   - o   15 años
   - o   16 años
   - o   17 años

3. ¿En dónde naciste?
   - o   Sinaloa
   - o   Ciudad de México
   - o   Otro estado de México
   - o   Fuera de México

4. ¿Qué tan satisfecho te encuentras con la forma en que te está yendo en la escuela?
   - o   Muy satisfecho
   - o   Algo satisfecho
   - o   Algo insatisfecho
   - o   Muy insatisfecho

5. Te consideras un alumno de
   - o   9-10 (nueve a diez)
   - o   8 (ocho)
   - o   7 (siete)
   - o   6 (seis)
   - o   5 (cinco)

6. ¿Piensas que en el futuro no te meterás en problemas?
   - o   Si
   - o   No
   - o   No sé

¿QUÉ PIENSAS?

Por favor indica qué tanto estás de acuerdo o en desacuerdo con estas afirmaciones sobre tu escuela.

7. La tarea es una pérdida de tiempo.
   - o   Muy de acuerdo

○ De acuerdo
○ En desacuerdo
○ Muy en desacuerdo

8. Me esfuerzo mucho en la escuela.
   ○ Muy de acuedo
   ○ De acuerdo
   ○ En desacuerdo
   ○ Muy en desacuerdo

9. La educación es tan importante que vale la pena aguantar las cosas de la escuela que no me gustan.
   ○ Muy de acuerdo
   ○ De acuerdo
   ○ En desacuerdo
   ○ Muy en desacuerdo

10. En términos generales, me gusta la escuela.
    ○ Muy de acuerdo
    ○ De acuerdo
    ○ En desacuerdo
    ○ Muy en desacuerdo

11. No me importa lo que los maestros piensan de mí.
    ○ Muy de acuerdo
    ○ De acuerdo
    ○ En desacuerdo
    ○ Muy en desacuerdo

12. Me preocupa la seguridad en mi colonia.
    ○ Nunca
    ○ Rara vez
    ○ Algunas veces
    ○ Seguido
    ○ Siempre

13. Me preocupo por mi seguridad al ir y venir de la escuela.
    ○ Nunca
    ○ Rara vez
    ○ Algunas veces
    ○ Seguido
    ○ Siempre

14. Me preocupo por mi seguridad al interior de la escuela.
    - o Nunca
    - o Rara vez
    - o Algunas veces
    - o Seguido
    - o Siempre

15. Observo actos de pandillas en mi colonia.
    - o Nunca
    - o Rara vez
    - o Algunas veces
    - o Seguido
    - o Siempre

¿Qué tan de acuerdo estás con las siguientes afirmaciones?

16. Si una persona no es exitosa en la vida es culpa suya.
    - o Muy de acuerdo
    - o De acuerdo
    - o En desacuerdo
    - o Muy en desacuerdo

17. Incluso contando con una buena educación, me costará trabajo encontrar el trabajo adecuado.
    - o Muy de acuerdo
    - o De acuerdo
    - o En desacuerdo
    - o Muy en desacuerdo

18. Gente como yo no tiene mucha oportunidad en la vida.
    - o Muy de acuerdo
    - o De acuerdo
    - o En desacuerdo
    - o Muy en desacuerdo

19. Si me meto en problemas es cuestión de suerte.
    - o Muy de acuerdo
    - o De acuerdo
    - o En desacuerdo
    - o Muy en desacuerdo

20. En gran medida puedo decidir lo que pasará en mi vida.
    o   Muy de acuerdo
    o   De acuerdo
    o   En desacuerdo
    o   Muy en desacuerdo

21. Es difícil salir adelante sin de vez en cuando violar la ley.
    o   Muy de acuerdo
    o   De acuerdo
    o   En desacuerdo
    o   Muy en desacuerdo

22. Si me quiero arriesgar a meter en problemas ese es mi asunto y de nadie más.
    o   Muy de acuerdo
    o   De acuerdo
    o   En desacuerdo
    o   Muy en desacuerdo

23. Yo no debo nada a mi comunidad.
    o   Muy de acuerdo
    o   De acuerdo
    o   En desacuerdo
    o   Muy en desacuerdo

24. Lo que haga con mi vida no hará mucha diferencia de una u otra forma.
    o   Muy de acuerdo
    o   De acuerdo
    o   En desacuerdo
    o   Muy en desacuerdo

25. De verdad me importa cómo mis actos pueden afectar a los demás.
    o   Muy de acuerdo
    o   De acuerdo
    o   En desacuerdo
    o   Muy en desacuerdo

26. Si estableces metas realistas puedes alcanzarlas.
    o   Muy en desacuerdo
    o   En desacuerdo

    o   De acuerdo

    o   Muy de acuerdo

27. Reprobar un ejercicio es muestra de una falta de esfuerzo suficiente de mi parte.

    o   Muy en desacuerdo

    o   En desacuerdo

    o   De acuerdo

    o   Muy de acuerdo

28. Si estudio lo suficientemente fuerte puedo salir bien en los exámenes.

    o   Muy en desacuerdo

    o   En desacuerdo

    o   De acuerdo

    o   Muy de acuerdo

29. Muchas cosas malas pasan en la vida de uno simplemente por mala suerte.

    o   Muy en desacuerdo

    o   En desacuerdo

    o   De acuerdo

    o   Muy de acuerdo

30. Una persona es responsable de sus acciones, buenas o malas.

    o   Muy en desacuerdo

    o   En desacuerdo

    o   De acuerdo

    o   Muy de acuerdo

31. Puedo quejarme de la política pero es casi todo lo que puedo hacer.

    o   Muy en desacuerdo

    o   En desacuerdo

    o   De acuerdo

    o   Muy de acuerdo

32. Yo salgo bien en la escuela porque trabajo duro, soy inteligente tengo aptitud.

    o   Muy en desacuerdo

    o   En desacuerdo

    o   De acuerdo

    o   Muy de acuerdo

33. Una persona puede cambiar su personalidad y comportamiento.
    o Muy en desacuerdo
    o En desacuerdo
    o De acuerdo
    o Muy de acuerdo

34. Mis acciones hoy definirán mi futuro.
    o Muy en desacuerdo
    o En desacuerdo
    o De acuerdo
    o Muy de acuerdo

35. Una persona no puede ascender más que su medio.
    o Muy en desacuerdo
    o En desacuerdo
    o De acuerdo
    o Muy de acuerdo

36. La delincuencia y la violencia pueden ser abolidas si la gente está convencida de lograrlo.
    o Muy en desacuerdo
    o En desacuerdo
    o De acuerdo
    o Muy de acuerdo

37. Tengo la responsabilidad de hacer del mundo un mejor lugar.
    o Muy de acuerdo
    o De acuerdo
    o En desacuerdo
    o Muy en desacuerdo

Las siguientes preguntas indagan "qué tan seguido" te sientes de una manera determinada.

38. Soy tan popular como otras personas de mi edad.
    o Nunca
    o Rara vez
    o Algunas veces
    o Seguido
    o Siempre

39. Desearía ser una persona diferente.
    o   Nunca
    o   Rara vez
    o   Algunas veces
    o   Seguido
    o   Siempre

40. Siento que en mi hogar las personas me prestan atención.
    o   Nunca
    o   Rara vez
    o   Algunas veces
    o   Seguido
    o   Siempre

41. Al salir de la *secundaria*, obtendré un trabajo que en verdad quiera.
    o   Nunca
    o   Rara vez
    o   Algunas veces
    o   Seguido
    o   Siempre

Las preguntas a continuación indagan lo que piensas sobre la policía.

42. En conjunto, ¿qué tan buen trabajo está realizando la policía?
    Está realizando..........
    o   Un muy buen trabajo
    o   Un buen trabajo
    o   Un trabajo a medias
    o   Un mal trabajo
    o   Un trabajo muy malo

43. Algunas personas dicen que la policía trata a todos de igual manera; otras, que favorece a unas personas sobre otras. ¿Y tu qué piensas? ¿Crees que la policía...
    o   Trata a todos de igual manera
    o   Favorece a unas personas sobre otras
    o   No sé

44. Si pidiera ayuda a la policía, ¿qué tan seguido me ofrecerían un buen servicio?
    o   Siempre

- o   Usualmente
- o   Algunas veces
- o   Rara vez
- o   No sé

45. Cuando los ciudadanos tratan con la policía, ¿qué tan seguido obtienen resultados justos?
- o   Siempre
- o   Usualmente
- o   Algunas veces
- o   Rara vez
- o   No sé

Las personas tienen opiniones diferentes respecto a qué tan importante es obedecer las leyes, a los oficiales de policía y a los jueces. Las siguientes preguntas tienen como fin conocer tus sentimientos sobre el obedecer la ley.

46. Las personas deben obeder la ley incluso si va en contra de lo que piensan es correcto.
- o   Muy de acuerdo
- o   De acuerdo
- o   En desacuerdo
- o   Muy en desacuerdo

47. Yo siempre trato de respetar la ley incluso cuando creo que está mal.
- o   Muy de acuerdo
- o   De acuerdo
- o   En desacuerdo
- o   Muy en desacuerdo

48. El desobedecer la ley rara vez tiene justificación.
- o   Muy de acuerdo
- o   De acuerdo
- o   En desacuerdo
- o   Muy en desacuerdo

49. Es difícil violar la ley y mantener el respeto de mí mismo.
- o   Muy de acuerdo
- o   De acuerdo
- o   En desacuerdo
- o   Muy en desacuerdo

50. No hay razón suficiente para que una persona como yo respete la ley.
    - o   Muy de acuerdo
    - o   De acuerdo
    - o   En desacuerdo
    - o   Muy en desacuerdo

51. Es difícil culpar a una persona por violar la ley si puede salirse con la suya.
    - o   Muy de acuerdo
    - o   De acuerdo
    - o   En desacuerdo
    - o   Muy en desacuerdo

52. Si una persona va ante el juez por una disputa con otra persona, y el juez le ordena pagar dinero al acusado, el demandante debe pagar al acusado el dinero aunque piense que el juez está equivocado.
    - o   Muy de acuerdo
    - o   De acuerdo
    - o   En desacuerdo
    - o   Muy en desacuerdo

53. Si una persona está haciendo algo y un oficial de policía le dice que pare, esta persona debe de parar aunque sienta que eso que está haciendo es legal.
    - o   Muy de acuerdo
    - o   De acuerdo
    - o   En desacuerdo
    - o   Muy en desacuerdo

En cada una de las preguntas a continuación, ¿con cuál afirmación estás <u>más</u> de acuerdo? Puedes estar de acuerdo con más de una pero ¿con cuál te identificas <u>más</u>?

54. Las personas **deben** cumplir la ley:
    - o   Para conservar el orden en la sociedad
    - o   Para obtener beneficios para todos
    - o   Para evitar ser castigado

55. Las personas **respetan** la ley:
    - o   Para conservar el orden en la sociedad

    o   Para obtener beneficios para todos
    o   Para evitar ser castigado

56. El motivo central de la ley es:
    o   El proteger los derechos de todos
    o   El obtener beneficios para todos
    o   El evitar conductas antisociales

57. Una ley justa es aquella que:
    o   Garantiza que todos obtendrán los mismos beneficios
    o   Ofrece el mayor beneficio a un mayor número de personas
    o   Garantiza que todos compartirán los beneficios y los costos

58. Las personas deben contar con derechos que:
    o   Sustenten su sistema legal y modo de vida
    o   Les permitan hacer lo que deseen
    o   Sean consistentes con los mejores intereses de todos

59. Debe ser apropiado violar una ley:
    o   Cuando siento que me va a beneficiar
    o   Cuando la ley es injusta
    o   Cuando hay una emergencia

60. Una ley justa es aquella que:
    o   Cuenta con el consenso de todos
    o   Mantiene a las personas fuera de problema
    o   Cuida de los jóvenes, inocentes y pobres

61. Si no existieran leyes, las personas:
    o   Notarían un aumento en el crimen, la violencia y el desorden
    o   Se moderarían a sí mismas
    o   Crearían nuevas leyes

62. Una ley puede ser modificada cuando:
    o   Las personas que la modifican se desempeñan en cargos con responsabilidad de crear o modificar leyes
    o   Las personas que la modifican cuentan con el poder suficiente para imponer su voluntad
    o   Las personas que la modifican piensan que la ley es injusta

63. Las personas pueden tener razón y violar la ley cuando:
    o   Sus razones e intereses son buenos
    o   La ley es injusta
    o   Es lo mejor para alcanzar lo que quieren o necesitan

64. Un derecho es:
    o   Algo que garantiza que las personas obtengan lo que quieren
    o   Un camino legal para garantizar los mismos privilegios para todos
    o   Una protección para que las garantías y libertades no sean usurpadas por las personas poderosas

¿QUÉ HAY DE TI?

En los últimos 60 días, ¿cuántas veces... ... ...

65. ... dañaste o destruiste intencionalmente propiedad ajena?
    o   Ninguna
    o   1 ó 2 veces
    o   3 ó 4 veces
    o   5 o más veces

66. ... robaste (o intentaste robar) algo de mucho valor?
    o   Ninguna
    o   1 ó 2 veces
    o   3 ó 4 veces
    o   5 o más veces

67. ... atacaste a alguien con la seria intención de lastimarlo(a) o matarlo(a)?
    o   Ninguna
    o   1 ó 2 veces
    o   3 ó 4 veces
    o   5 o más veces

68. ... participaste en peleas?
    o   Ninguna
    o   1 ó 2 veces
    o   3 ó 4 veces
    o   5 o más veces

69. ... evitaste pagar por cosas como tu entrada al cine, la tarifa del camión o tu comida?
    o Ninguna
    o 1 ó 2 veces
    o 3 ó 4 veces
    o 5 o más veces

70. ... usaste la fuerza (represiva) para obtener dinero o las pertenencias de otra persona, como por ejemplo el dinero de uno de tus compañeros de escuela?
    o Ninguna
    o 1 ó 2 veces
    o 3 ó 4 veces
    o 5 o más veces

En los últimos 60 días, ¿cuántos de tus amigos con los que pasas la mayor parte del tiempo...

71. ... sugirieron que hicieras algo que va en contra de la ley?
    o Todos
    o La mayoría
    o Unos cuantos
    o Ninguno

72. ... terminaron casi toda su tarea?
    o Todos
    o La mayoría
    o Unos cuantos
    o Ninguno

73. ... dañaron o destruyeron propiedad ajena?
    o Todos
    o La mayoría
    o Unos cuantos
    o Ninguno

74. ... participaron en actividades religiosas como ir a la iglesia?
    o Todos
    o La mayoría
    o Unos cuantos
    o Ninguno

75. ... estuvieron involucrados en actos de pandilla?
    o   Todos
    o   La mayoría
    o   Unos cuantos
    o   Ninguno

76. ... pararon una pelea?
    o   Todos
    o   La mayoría
    o   Unos cuantos
    o   Ninguno

77. ... golpearon o amenazaron con golpear a alguna persona?
    o   Todos
    o   La mayoría
    o   Unos cuantos
    o   Ninguno

Para cada una de las siguientes preguntas, elige la respuesta más correcta.

En las preguntas 78 a 80 escoge el mejor significado para cada una de las preguntas

78. Libre albedrío:
    o   Incitar a las personas a realizar ciertas acciones o alejarlas de cometerlas
    o   Rasgos de carácter y comportamiento intrínsecos que hacen únicas a las personas
    o   Capacidad de tomar decisiones y elegir comportamientos
    o   Sentimientos que uno tiene sobre sí mismo
    o   No sé

79. Naturaleza humana:
    o   Incitar a las personas a realizar ciertas acciones o alejarlas de cometerlas
    o   Rasgos de carácter y comportamiento intrínsecos que hacen únicas a las personas
    o   Capacidad de tomar decisiones y elegir comportamientos
    o   Sentimientos que uno tiene sobre sí mismo
    o   No sé

80. Auto estima:
    o   Incitar a las personas a realizar ciertas acciones o alejarlas de cometerlas
    o   Rasgos de carácter y comportamiento intrínsecos que hacen únicas a las personas
    o   Capacidad de tomar decisiones y elegir comportamientos
    o   Sentimientos que uno tiene sobre sí mismo
    o   No sé

81. El valor de una persona NO debe ser decidido por sus:
    o   Posesiones materiales
    o   Bondad hacia los demás
    o   Compasión
    o   Contribuciones a la sociedad
    o   No sé

82. El cometer un acto prohibido por la ley se conoce como:
    o   Delito
    o   Proceso justo
    o   Corrupción
    o   Castigo
    o   No sé

83. Si un oficial de la policía acepta un pago a cambio de voltear para el otro lado mientras que un pandillero vende drogas, el oficial de la policía está:
    o   Tomando lo que con razón es suyo
    o   Respetando el estado de derecho
    o   Realizando un acto de "proceso justo"
    o   Realizando un acto de corrupción
    o   Todas las anteriores

84. El convertirse en delincuente no es una decisión que generalmente se toma de la noche a la mañana, sino un lento descenso durante un periodo de tiempo largo.
    o   Cierto
    o   Falso
    o   No sé

85. Las personas que participan en actividades criminales afectan:
    o   A la sociedad en general
    o   Sus propias vidas

o   Sus familias y sus víctimas
o   Todas las anteriores
o   No sé

86. En una cultura de legalidad existen TODAS las siguientes características, con EXCEPCIÓN de una. ¿Cuál característica NO pertenece?

o   Existe un sistema estructurado de proceso justo para aquellos que violan la ley
o   Las personas en la sociedad no pueden modificar las leyes de una u otra forma
o   La mayoría de las personas están dispuestas a respetar las normas y leyes
o   La cultura rechaza al crimen y la corrupción
o   Existe un cuerpo estructurado de procuración de justicia y un conjunto de castigos formales para los que violan la ley

87. En *El señor de las moscas* el intento del niño (Ralph) de crear un orden al convocar una reunión para elaborar reglas es un ejemplo de intento de:

o   Establecer el estado de derecho
o   Exentarse de seguir las reglas
o   Convertirse en dictador
o   Integrar una pandilla
o   No sé

88. A una sociedad que cuenta con un conjunto sólido de leyes, donde las personas buscan salir de problemas ofreciendo dinero, y aquellos en el poder pueden hacer lo que quieren, se le conoce como una sociedad:

o   Sin estado de derecho
o   Con una cultura de legalidad
o   Con estado de derecho
o   b y c
o   No sé

89. Es apropiado no respetar la ley y cometer desobediencia civil cuando:

o   Una ley es injusta, todos los esfuerzos legales para modificarla han fallado y estoy preparado a pagar las consecuencias
o   Siempre que la ley se interponga a mis planes

    o   Nunca es lo correcto porque uno nunca debe violar la ley
    o   Cuando mis amigos me dicen que una ley es absurda, y amenazan con no ser más mis amigos si decido respetarla

90. En ocasiones, el crimen y la corrupción son exitosos porque:
    o   Las personas se sienten intimidadas y no tienen a quien voltear para protección
    o   Los individuos desean algunos de los servicios que el crimen y la corrupción ofrecen ilegalmente
    o   Oficiales corruptos permiten que las actividades criminales se desarrollen
    o   Todas las anteriores
    o   No sé

91. Las acciones de hoy _____
    o   No importan cuando eres menor de edad
    o   Pueden tener consecuencias bien entrado el futuro
    o   Eventualmente desaparecerán
    o   Todas las anteriores
    o   No sé

92. La solución de problemas es
    o   Una "destreza para la vida" importante porque el no prestar atención o intentar resolver los problemas puede empeorarlos
    o   No es una "destreza para la vida" importante porque yo debo aceptar mi vida tal y como es, y no hacer nada para cambiarla
    o   No es una "destreza para la vida" importante porque cuento con mis amigos y familia para que resuelvan mis problemas
    o   Es una "destreza para la vida" importante porque me hará rico(a)
    o   No sé

93. Si tus amigos(as) te dicen que robes goma de mascar de la tienda de la esquina
    o   Es lo apropiado porque no se hará daño alguno al dueño de la tienda si no se le paga una pieza de goma de mascar
    o   Es lo apropiado porque si eres lo suficientemente inteligente y veloz no te van a atrapar
    o   No es lo apropiado porque si tus papás se enteran te puedes meter en problemas

     o   No es lo apropiado porque debes respetar la propiedad del dueño de la tienda

     o   No sé

94. En una sociedad caracterizada por el estado de derecho:
     o   Se supone que las leyes se aplican a todos
     o   El gobernante y los ricos no tienen que respetar las leyes
     o   Las leyes se aplican a juicio de la policía
     o   La gente es dominada por el gobernante
     o   No sé

95. El resultado final de tolerar hasta pequeñas violaciones a la ley de parte mía o la de otros es
     o   Una falta absoluta de consideración por los derechos individuales de una sociedad
     o   Un estado sin leyes
     o   No hay nada que guíe el comportamiento de los individuos
     o   Todas las anteriores
     o   No sé

96. La responsabilidad de combatir al crimen organizado y la corrupción descansa sobre:
     o   La comunidad
     o   Las fuerzas locales de procuración de justicia
     o   El gobierno federal
     o   Todas las anteriores

97. Si la policía respetara el estado de derecho, ¿la apoyarías?
     o   Si
     o   No
     o   No sé

APPENDIX B

STUDENT SURVEY

Name of School: **Date:**

Name of Teacher: **Class Period:**

We want to know how you feel about your school, yourself, and your activities. We need your honest answers to the following questions. We want to find out what students in your school think and do. There are no right and wrong answers. **This is NOT a test.**

We do not want your name on your answer sheet. Your answers are **CONFIDENTIAL.** The answers of many students will be averaged to describe your school.

One more thing – please do not talk or compare answers. If you have any questions at any time, raise your hand. Please circle the best answer for each question. This survey will be given in two parts during this and the next class

---

WHO ARE YOU?

1. Are you:
    - ○ Female
    - ○ Male

2. How old are you?
    - ○ 13 years old
    - ○ 14 years old
    - ○ 15 years old
    - ○ 16 years old
    - ○ 17 years old

3. How do you describe yourself?
    - ○ Georgian
    - ○ Armenian
    - ○ Azeri
    - ○ Turkish
    - ○ Other

4. How satisfied are you with the way you are doing in school?
    - ○ Very satisfied
    - ○ Somewhat satisfied
    - ○ Somewhat dissatisfied
    - ○ Very dissatisfied

5. Would you say you are currently an
    - ○ A student
    - ○ B student
    - ○ C student
    - ○ D student
    - ○ F student

6. What grade are you in?
    - ○ 7th Grade
    - ○ 8th Grade
    - ○ 9th Grade
    - ○ 10th Grade
    - ○ 11th Grade
    - ○ 12th Grade

7. Do you think you will stay out of trouble in the future?
   o Yes
   o No
   o Don't know

WHAT DO YOU THINK?

Please indicate how much you agree or disagree with these statements about your school.

8. Homework is a waste of time
   o Strongly agree
   o Agree
   o Disagree
   o Strongly disagree

9. I try hard in school.
   o Strongly agree
   o Agree
   o Disagree
   o Strongly disagree

10. Education is so important that it's worth it to put up with things about school that I don't like.
    o Strongly agree
    o Agree
    o Disagree
    o Strongly disagree

11. In general, I like school.
    o Strongly agree
    o Agree
    o Disagree
    o Strongly disagree

12. I don't care what teachers think about me.
    o Strongly agree
    o Agree
    o Disagree
    o Strongly disagree

13. I worry about safety in my neighborhood.
    - o Never
    - o Seldom
    - o Sometimes
    - o Often
    - o Always

14. I worry about my safety getting to and from school.
    - o Never
    - o Seldom
    - o Sometimes
    - o Often
    - o Always

15. I worry about my safety in school.
    - o Never
    - o Seldom
    - o Sometimes
    - o Often
    - o Always

16. I see gang activity in my neighborhood.
    - o Never
    - o Seldom
    - o Sometimes
    - o Often
    - o Always

How much do you agree?

17. If a person is not a success in life, it is his own fault.
    - o Strongly agree
    - o Agree
    - o Disagree
    - o Strongly disagree

18. Even with a good education, I'll have a hard time getting the right kind of job.
    - o Strongly agree
    - o Agree
    - o Disagree
    - o Strongly disagree

19. People like me don't have much of a chance in life.
    - o   Strongly agree
    - o   Agree
    - o   Disagree
    - o   Strongly disagree
20. Whether I get into trouble is just a matter of chance.
    - o   Strongly agree
    - o   Agree
    - o   Disagree
    - o   Strongly disagree

21. I can pretty much decide what will happen in my life.
    - o   Strongly agree
    - o   Agree
    - o   Disagree
    - o   Strongly disagree

22. It is hard to get ahead without breaking the law now and then.
    - o   Strongly agree
    - o   Agree
    - o   Disagree
    - o   Strongly disagree

23. If I want to risk getting into trouble, that is my business and nobody else's
    - o   Strongly agree
    - o   Agree
    - o   Disagree
    - o   Strongly disagree

24. I don't owe the world anything.
    - o   Strongly agree
    - o   Agree
    - o   Disagree
    - o   Strongly disagree

25. What I do with my life won't make much difference one way or the other.
    - o   Strongly agree
    - o   Agree
    - o   Disagree
    - o   Strongly disagree

26. I really care about how my actions might affect others.
    - o Strongly agree
    - o Agree
    - o Disagree
    - o Strongly disagree

27. Chance has nothing to do with being successful.
    - o Strongly disagree
    - o Disagree
    - o Agree
    - o Strongly agree

28. Whatever plans you make, there is always something that will cross them.
    - o Strongly disagree
    - o Disagree
    - o Agree
    - o Strongly agree

29. Being at the right place, at the right time is essential for getting what you want in life.
    - o Strongly disagree
    - o Disagree
    - o Agree
    - o Strongly agree

30. You cannot fool your destiny.
    - o Strongly disagree
    - o Disagree
    - o Agree
    - o Strongly agree

31. If you set realistic goals, you can succeed no matter what.
    - o Strongly disagree
    - o Disagree
    - o Agree
    - o Strongly agree

32. Many people lead miserable lives because of their parents.
    - o Strongly disagree
    - o Disagree
    - o Agree
    - o Strongly agree

33. Failing an assignment is a sign of insufficient effort on my part.
    - o Strongly disagree
    - o Disagree
    - o Agree
    - o Strongly agree

34. If I study hard enough, I can succeed on any exam.
    - o Strongly disagree
    - o Disagree
    - o Agree
    - o Strongly agree

35. Many bad things in one's life happen just because of bad luck.
    - o Strongly disagree
    - o Disagree
    - o Agree
    - o Strongly agree

36. A person is responsible for her/his own actions, good or bad.
    - o Strongly disagree
    - o Disagree
    - o Agree
    - o Strongly agree

37. I can complain about politics, but that's about all I can do.
    - o Strongly disagree
    - o Disagree
    - o Agree
    - o Strongly agree

38. I succeed at school because I am capable, intelligent or skilled.
    - o Strongly disagree
    - o Disagree
    - o Agree
    - o Strongly agree

39. A person can change his/her personality and behavior patterns.
    - o Strongly disagree
    - o Disagree
    - o Agree
    - o Strongly agree

40. One reaps the harvest of one's own actions.
    - o   Strongly disagree
    - o   Disagree
    - o   Agree
    - o   Strongly agree

41. A person cannot rise above his/her background.
    - o   Strongly disagree
    - o   Disagree
    - o   Agree
    - o   Strongly agree

42. Crime and violence can be abolished if people set their mind to it.
    - o   Strongly disagree
    - o   Disagree
    - o   Agree
    - o   Strongly agree

43. People make a difference in controlling crime.
    - o   Strongly disagree
    - o   Disagree
    - o   Agree
    - o   Strongly agree

44. I have a responsibility to make the world a better place.
    - o   Strongly agree
    - o   Agree
    - o   Disagree
    - o   Strongly disagree

The next questions ask you to circle "how often" you feel a particular way.

45. I am as popular as other people my age.
    - o   Never
    - o   Seldom
    - o   Sometimes
    - o   Often
    - o   Always

46. I wish I were a different person.
    - o Never
    - o Seldom
    - o Sometimes
    - o Often
    - o Always

47. I feel like people pay attention to me at home.
    - o Never
    - o Seldom
    - o Sometimes
    - o Often
    - o Always

48. After high school, I will get a job I really want.
    - o Never
    - o Seldom
    - o Sometimes
    - o Often
    - o Always

The next questions ask about your attitudes toward the police.

49. Overall, how good a job are the police doing? Are they doing..........
    - o A very good job
    - o A good job
    - o A fair job
    - o A poor job
    - o A very poor job

50. Some people say that the police treat everyone equally, others that they favor some people over others. How about you, do you think that the police......
    - o Treat everyone equally
    - o They favor some people over others.
    - o Don't know

51. In general, when people call the police for assistance, how often do you think that the police provide them with satisfactory service?

  o   Always
  o   Usually
  o   Sometimes
  o   Seldom
  o   Don't know

52. How often do the citizens receive fair outcomes when they deal with the police?
  o   Always
  o   Usually
  o   Sometimes
  o   Seldom
  o   Don't know

People have different opinions about how important it is to obey police officers, judges, and the law. The following questions are concerned with your own feelings about obeying the law.

53. People should obey the law even if it goes against what they think is right.
  o   Agree strongly
  o   Agree
  o   Disagree
  o   Strongly disagree

54. I always try to follow the law even if I think that it is wrong.
  o   Agree strongly
  o   Agree
  o   Disagree
  o   Strongly disagree

55. Disobeying the law is seldom justified.
  o   Agree strongly
  o   Agree
  o   Disagree
  o   Strongly disagree

56. It is difficult to break the law and keep one's self-respect.
  o   Agree strongly
  o   Agree
  o   Disagree
  o   Strongly disagree

57. There is very little reason for a person like me to obey the law.
    - ○ Agree strongly
    - ○ Agree
    - ○ Disagree
    - ○ Strongly disagree

58. It is hard to blame a person for breaking the law if they can get away with it.
    - ○ Agree strongly
    - ○ Agree
    - ○ Disagree
    - ○ Strongly disagree

59. If a person goes to court because of a dispute with another person, and the judge orders them to pay the other person money, they should pay that person money, even if they think that the judge is wrong.
    - ○ Agree strongly
    - ○ Agree
    - ○ Disagree
    - ○ Strongly disagree

60. If a person is doing something and a police officer tells them to stop, they should stop even if they feel that what they are doing is legal.
    - ○ Agree strongly
    - ○ Agree
    - ○ Disagree
    - ○ Strongly disagree

For each of the following questions, which statement do you most agree with?

61. People **should** follow the law:
    - ○ to maintain order for society
    - ○ to gain benefits for all
    - ○ to avoid being punished

62. People **do** follow the law:
    - ○ to maintain order for society
    - ○ to gain benefits for all
    - ○ to avoid being punished

63. The main reason for law is:
    - o   to secure rights for all
    - o   to gain benefits for all
    - o   to prevent anti-social behavior

64. A fair law is one that:
    - o   assures that everyone will get the same benefits
    - o   does the most good for the most people
    - o   assures that everyone will share benefits and burdens

65. People should have rights that:
    - o   maintain their legal system and way of life
    - o   allow them to do what they want
    - o   are consistent with the best interests of all

66. It must be right to break a law:
    - o   When I feel like it will benefit me
    - o   When the law is unfair
    - o   When there is an emergency

67. A fair law is one that:
    - o   has everyone's agreement
    - o   keeps people out of trouble
    - o   takes care of the young, innocent, and poor

68. If there were no laws, people would:
    - o   see an increase in crime, violence, and disorder
    - o   regulate themselves
    - o   make new laws

69. A law can be changed when:
    - o   people changing it have a law-making or changing role
    - o   people changing it have enough power to enforce their will
    - o   people changing it think that the law is unfair

70. People can be right and break the law when:
    - o   their motives and interests are good.
    - o   The law is unjust
    - o   It is best for getting them what they want or need.

71. A right is:
    - o   something that assures people of getting what they want.
    - o   a legal way to guarantee equal privileges for everyone.
    - o   a protection of freedoms and liberties from being taken away by the powerful.

WHAT ABOUT YOU?

In the last 60 days, how many times.................

72. Purposely damage or destroy property that did not belong to you?
    - o   Never
    - o   1 or 2 times
    - o   3 or 4 times
    - o   5 or more times

73. Stolen (or tried to steal) something worth a lot of money?
    - o   Never
    - o   1 or 2 times
    - o   3 or 4 times
    - o   5 or more times

74. Attacked someone with the idea of seriously hurting or killing him or her?
    - o   Never
    - o   1 or 2 times
    - o   3 or 4 times
    - o   5 or more times

75. Been involved in fights anywhere?
    - o   Never
    - o   1 or 2 times
    - o   3 or 4 times
    - o   5 or more times

76. Avoided paying for such things as movies, subway rides, or food?
    - o   Never
    - o   1 or 2 times
    - o   3 or 4 times
    - o   5 or more times

77. Used force (strong-armed) to get money or things from other people?
    - o   Never
    - o   1 or 2 times
    - o   3 or 4 times
    - o   5 or more times

Over the past 60 days, how many of the friends you spend most of your time with…..

78. Suggested that you do something that was against the law?
    - o   All
    - o   Most
    - o   a few
    - o   none

79. Did nearly all of their homework?
    - o   All
    - o   Most
    - o   a few
    - o   none

80. Damaged or destroyed property that did not belong to them?
    - o   All
    - o   Most
    - o   a few
    - o   none

81. Participated in religious activities like going to church?
    - o   All
    - o   Most
    - o   a few
    - o   none

82. were involved in gang activities?
    - o   All
    - o   Most
    - o   a few
    - o   none

83. Stopped a fight?
    - o   All
    - o   Most
    - o   a few
    - o   none

84. Hit or threatened to hit someone?
    - o   All
    - o   Most
    - o   a few
    - o   none

For each of the following, circle the most correct answer.

For Questions 85 to 87 circle the best definition for each of the questions provided.

85. Free will:
    - o   Push or people toward or away from certain actions.
    - o   Fundamental character traits and behavior that make people unique.
    - o   Ability to make decisions and choose behavior.
    - o   Feelings one has about oneself.
    - o   I don't know.

86. Human nature:
    - o   Push or people toward or away from certain actions.
    - o   Fundamental character traits and behavior that make people unique.
    - o   Ability to make decisions and choose behavior.
    - o   Feelings one has about oneself.
    - o   I don't know.

87. Self esteem:
    - o   Push or people toward or away from certain actions.
    - o   Fundamental character traits and behavior that make people unique.
    - o   Ability to make decisions and choose behavior.
    - o   Feelings one has about oneself.
    - o   I don't know.

88. A person's worth should NOT be determined by their:
    - material possessions
    - kindness to others
    - compassion
    - contributions to society
    - I don't know.

89. Committing an act forbidden by law or failing to do something required by law is known as:
    - corruption
    - due process
    - crime
    - punishment
    - I don't know

90. If a police officer is paid money to look the other way while a bodega owner serves alcohol to minors, he or she is engaging in an act of:
    - corruption
    - due process
    - value
    - punishment
    - I don't know

91. Becoming a criminal is usually not an overnight decision, but rather a slow descent over a long period of time.
    - True
    - False
    - I don't know

92. People engaged in criminal activity affect:
    - Only society
    - Only themselves
    - Only their families and their victims
    - Everyone
    - I don't know

93. Which of the following is a characteristic of a "culture of lawfulness"?
    - criminal acts are accepted
    - criminals are admired
    - parts/all of the legal system are corrupt
    - people report crime and are willing to testify in court
    - I don't know.

94. Crime and corruption are at times successful because:
    - o   people are intimidated and they have no one to turn to for protection
    - o   individuals want some of the services illegally provided by crime and corruption
    - o   corrupt officials allow criminal activity to take place
    - o   all of the above
    - o   I don't know

95. Present actions_____
    - o   Don't matter when you are a minor
    - o   Can have consequences far into the future
    - o   Will eventually go away
    - o   Should not concern others
    - o   I don't know

BIBLIOGRAPHY

Adelson, J., Green, and R. O'Neil (1966). "The development of political thought in adolescence: the sense of community". *Journal of Personality and Social Psychology,* 4, (August), 295-306.

Akers, R. (1985). *Deviant Behavior: a Social Learning Approach.* 3rd edition. Belmont, CA: Wadsworth Publishing Co.

Akers, R., M. Krohn, L. Lonza-Kaduce, and M. Radosevich (1979). "Social learning and deviant behavior: a specific test of general theory". *American Sociological Review,* 44, 635-655.

Allport (1961). *Pattern and Growth in Personality.* New York: Holt, Rinehart, and Winston.

America's Watch Report (1990). *Human Rights in Mexico: a Policy of Impunity.* New York: Human Rights Watch.

Arbuckle, J. and W. Wothke (2003). *Amos 5.0 Update to the Amos User's Guide.* Chicago: Smallwaters Corporation.

Bahn, C. (1973). "The Counter Training Problem". *Personnel Journal,* December 1973, pp. 1068-1072.

Bandura, A. (1975). *Social Learning & Personality Development:* Holt, Rinehart & Winston, INC: NJ.

Bandura, A. (1969). "Self-efficacy: toward a unifying theory of behavioral change". *Psychological Review,* (2), pp. 191-215.

Barber, B. (2000). *A Passion for Democracy.* Princeton: Princeton University Press.

Baron, R. M., & Kenny, D. A. (1986). "The moderator-mediator variable distinction in social psychological research: Conceptual, strategic and statistical considerations". *Journal of Personality and Social Psychology*, 51, 1173-1182.

Baseheart, J. and T. Cox (1993). "Effects of police use of profanity on a receiver's perceptions of credibility". *Journal of Police and Criminal Psychology*, 9 (2), pp. 9-19.

Basinger, K. and J. Gibbs (1987). "Validation of the Sociomoral Reflection Objective Measure-Short Form". *Psychological Reports*, 61, 139-46.

Baumiester. (2001). "Violent Pride: Do people turn violent because of self-hate, or self-love". *Scientific American*, 284 (4), 96-101.

Blasi, A. (1980). "Bridging moral cognition and moral action: a critical review of the literature." *Psychological Bulletin*, 88, (1), pp. 1-45.

Blatt, M., and L. Kohlberg (1969). "The effects of classroom moral discussion on the development of moral judgment". In L. Kohlberg and E. Turiel (eds.). *Recent Research in Moral Judgment*. New York: Holt, Rinehart and Winston.

Block, J. & Kremen, A., (1996). "IQ and Ego-Resiliency: Conceptual and Empirical Connections and Separateness." Journal of Personality and Social Psychology, 70, 349-361.

Boyes, M., & Walker, L.J. (1988). Implications of cultural diversity for the universality claims of Kohlberg's theory of moral reasoning. *Human Development*, 31, 44-59

Brandt, D., and K. Markus (2001). "Adolescent attitudes towards the police: a new generation". *Journal of Police and Criminal Psychology*, 15 (1), pp. 10-16.

Brown, D. (1974). "Cognitive development and willingness to comply with the law". *American Journal of Political Science*, 18 (3), pp. 583-94.

Byrne, D. (1998). *Structural Equation Modeling with Amos: Basic Concepts, Applications, and Programming*. Mahweh: Lawrence Erlbaum Associates.

Camp, R. (1999). *Politics in Mexico: the Decline of Authoritarianism*. Oxford: Oxford University Press.

Center for Urban Affairs and Policy Research, Middle Schools Project (1995). *Adolescent Attitude Survey.* Houston, TX.

Chan, T (1998). "Corruption Prevention: the Hong Kong Experience". Unpublished paper. 113th International Training Course: Visiting Experts Papers.

Chevigny, P. (1999). "Defining the role of the police in Latin America". *The (Un)rule of Law.* Notre Dame: University of Notre Dame Press, pp 49-70.

Chorak, B. (1997). "Legal education for juveniles". *Corrections Today,* Vol. 59, 2, pp 152-156.

Cloward, R., and L. Ohlin. (1960). *Delinquency and Opportunity: a Theory of Delinquent Gangs.* New York: Free Press.

Cohn, E. and S. White. (1990). *Legal Socialization: a study of norms and rules.* New York, NY: Springer-Verlag.

Cohn, E., and S. White. (1992). "Taking reasoning seriously". In *Advances in Criminological Theory: Facts, Frameworks, and Forecasts.* J. McCord (ed.). New Brunswick: Transaction Publishers.

Cohn, E. and S. White (1997). "Legal socialization effects on democratization". *International Social Science Journal,* 152, pp 151-171.

Cohen, E. L.; Wyman, P. A.; Work, W. C.; and Parker, G. R. (1990). The Rochester child resilience project: Overview and summary of first year findings. Development and *Psychopathology,* 2, 193-212.

Damon, W. (1977). *The Social World of the Child.* San Francisco: Jossey-Bass.

Davis, J. (1974). "Justification for no obligation: views of black males toward crime and the criminal law." *Issues in Criminology,* 9, pp. 69-87.

Dewey, J. (1930). *Human Nature and Conduct.* New York: Modern Library

Dubow and Luster (1990). "Adjustment of children born to teenage mothers: the contribution of risk and protective factors". *Journal of Marriage and the Family,* 52 (2) (May 1990): 393-404.

Earls, F.J. (1994). "Violence and today's youth". *Critical Issues for Children and Youth,* 4, 4-23.

Elliott, D. (1994). "Serious violent offenders: onset, developmental course, and termination – the American Society of Criminology 1993 presidential address". *Criminology,* 32, pp. 1-21.

Embrey, D., A. Vazsonyi, K. Powell, and H. Atha (1996). "PeaceBuilders: a theoretically driven, school-based model for early violence prevention". *American Journal of Preventive Medicine,* 12, 91-100.

Farrington, D. (1989). "Early predictors of adolescent aggression and adult violence". *Violence and Victims,* 4, pp. 79-100.

Finckenauer, J. (1995). *Russian Youth: Law Deviance, and the Pursuit of Freedom.* New Brunwick, NJ: Transaction Publishers.

Finckenauer, J. (1998). "Legal socialization: concepts and practices". http://www.civnet.org/journal/issue5/ftjfinck.htm.

Fraser, M (1996). "Aggressive behavior in childhood and early adolescence: an ecological developmental perspective on youth violence". *Social Work,* 41, 347-361.

Freedman, M. (1988). *Partners in Growth: Elder Mentors and At-Risk Youth.* Executive Summary. Philadelphia, PA: Public/Private Ventures.

Friedrichs, D. (1986). "The concept of legitimation and the legal order: a response to Hyde's Critique," *Justice Quarterly,* 3:1, 35-50.

Fuller, Lon (1964). *The Morality of Law.* New Haven: Yale University Press.

Furnham, A. and B. Stacey (1991). *Young People's Understanding of Society.* London: Routledge.

Galindo, J. (2000). "Mexico kisses perfect dictatorship goodbye". *Thunderbird Online Magazine.* http://www.journalism.ubc.ca/thunderbird/2001-01/october/mexico.htm

Gardiner, L. (2002). Critique of the NSIC Culture of Lawfulness Trainin Program. Unpublished personal correspondence with the author.

Garmezy, N. (1991). Resilience in children's adaptation to negative life events and stressed environments. *Psychiatric Annals,* 20(9), 462-466.

Garmezy, N. (1993). Children in poverty: Resilience despite risk. *Psychiatry,* 56, 127-136.

Garmezy, N. & Masten, A. (1991). The protective role of competence indicators in children at risk. In E. M. Cummings, A. L. Greene, & K.

H. Karrakei (Eds.), *Perspectives on Stress and Coping* (pp. 151-174). Hillsdale, NJ: Erlbaum Associates.

Garrett, P., Ng'andu, N. and Ferron, J. (1994). "Poverty Experiences of Young Children and the Quality of their Home Environments". *Child Development,* 65(2): 331-45.

Garret (1995). Murder by Teens has Soared. New York Newsday. February 17.

Gibbs, J., K. Arnold, H. Ahlborn, and F. Cheesman. (1984). "Facilitation of sociomoral reasoning in delinquents". *Jouranal of Consulting and Clinical Psychology,* 52, 37-45.

Gibbs, J., K. Basinger, and D. Fuller (1992). *Moral Maturity: Measuring the Development of Sociomoral Reflection.* Hillsdale: Lawrence Erlbaum Associates.

Gibbs, J., Widaman, K., & Colby, A. (1982). Construction and Validation of a Simplified, Group-administerable Equivalent to the Moral Judgment Interview. *Child Development,* 53(4), 895.

Gibbs, N (2001). "A Whole New World". *Time Special Issue.* June 11, 2001.

Gibson, J. (1991). "Understandings of justice: institutional legitimacy, procedural justice, and political tolerance". *Law and Society Review,* 23 (3), pp. 469-96.

Gibson, J. and G. Caldiera (1996). "The legal cultures of Europe". *Law and Society Review,* 30, pp. 55-85.

Gibson, J., R. Duch, and K. Tedin (1992). "Democratic values and the transformation of the Soviet Union". *Journal of Politics,* 54, 329-371.

Gielen, U., H. Cruckshank, A. Johnston, B. Swanzey, and J. Avellani (1986). "The development of moral reasoning in Belize, Trinidad-Tobago, and the U.S.A." *Behavioral Science Research,* 20 (1-4), 178-207.

Gielen, U., and D. Markoulis (1994). "Preference for principled moral reasoning: a developmental and cross-cultural perspectives". In L. Adler and U. Gielen (ed.). *Cross-cultural Topics in Psychology.* Westport, CT: Greenwood.

Gilligan, C. (1982). *In a Difference Voice: Psychological Theory and Women's Development.* Cambridge, MA: Harvard University Press.

Godson, R. (1999). "Culture Matters and School-based Education Contributes to Culture". Washington, DC: National Strategy Information Center.

Godson, R. (2000). "Guide to Developing a Culture of Lawfulness". Unpublished paper prepared for the Symposium on the Role of Civil Society in Countering Organized Crime: Global Implications of the Palermo, Sicily Renaissance. December 14, 2000.

Godson, R. and D. Kenney (2000). *School-Based Education to Counter Crime and Corruption.* Washington, DC: National Strategy Information Center.

Gore, S. and Eckenrode, J. (1994) Context and process in research on risk and resilience. In R. Haggerty et al. (Eds.) *Stress, Risk and Resilience in Children and Adolescents: Processes, Mechanisms and Interventions.* New York: Cambridge University Press

Gottfredson, M., and T. Hirschi. (1990). *A General Theory of Crime.* Stanford: Stanford University Press.

Gottfredson, G. (1991). *The Effective School Battery: User's Manual.* Odessa: Psychological Assessment Resources.

Greenburg, M. and E. Wertlieb. (1985). "The police role in law-related education". *The Police Chief,* January 1995, pp. 34-41.

Guerra, N., L. Huesmann, P. Tolan, R. Acker, L. Eron (1995). "Stressful events and individual beliefs as correlates of economic disadvantage and aggression among urban children. *Journal of Consulting and Clinical Psychology,* 63, 518-528.

Hair, Anderson, Tatham, and Black (1999).

Harris, D. (2002). *Profiles in Injustice: why racial profiling cannot work.* New York: the New Press.

Hawkins, J., M. Arthur, R. Catalano (1995). "Preventing substance abuse". In *Building a Safer Society: Strategic Approaches to Crime Prevention: Vol. 19, Crime and Justice: A Review of Research.* M. Tonry and D. Farrington (eds.). Chicago, IL: University of Chicago Press, pp. 343-427.

Hawkins, J., R. Catalano, and J. Miller. (1992). "Risk and protective factors for alcohol and other drug problems in adolescence and early

adulthood: implications for substance abuse prevention".
Psychological Bulletin, 112, pp. 64-105.

Hawkins, J., T. Herrenkohl, D. Farrington, D. Brewer, R. Catalano, T. Harachi, and L. Cothern (2000). "Predictors of youth violence". *OJJDP Juvenile Justice Bulletin,* Washington, DC: U.S. Department of Justice.

Hess, R. and J. Tapp (1969). "Authority, rules, and aggression: a cross-national study of the socialization of children into compliance systems". Part I. Washington, D.C.: U.S. Office of Education.

Hirschi, T. (1969). *Causes of Delinquency.* Berkely, CA: University of California Press.

Hoyle, Rick H. (1995). Structural equation modeling : concepts, issues, and applications / Rick H. Hoyle, editor. , Thousand Oaks, Calif., Sage Publications.

Hu, L.-T., & Bentler, P. (1995). Evaluating model fit. In R. H. Hoyle (Ed.), *Structural Equation Modeling. Concepts, Issues, and Applications* (pp. 76-99). Calif., Sage Publications.

Institute of Behavioral Science. (1990). Youth Interview Schedule: Denver Youth Survey. Boulder, CO: University of Colorado, 1990.

Jacobson, M. and S. Palonsky" (1981). "Effects of a law-related education program". *The Elementary School Journal,* 82 (1), pp. 49-57.

Jerebek, I. (2000). *Locus of Control and Attribution Survey –Revised.* Body-Mind: Queendom.

Jesilow, P. and J. Meyer (2001). "The effect of police misconduct on public attitudes". *Journal of Crime and Justice,* 24, pp. 109-21.

Jones-Brown, D. (1996). *Race and Legal Socialization.* Unpublished dissertation: Rutgers, the State University of New Jersey.

Jones-Brown, D. (2000). "Debunking the myth of officer friendly: how African-American males experience community policing". *Journal of Contemporary Criminal Justice,* 16 (2), pp. 209-229.

Kaminski, R., and E. Jefferies. (1998). "The effect of a violent televised arrest on public perceptions of the police". *Policing: an international journal of police strategies and management,* 21 (4), pp. 683-706.

Kandel, E., and S. Mednick. (1991). "Perinatal complications predict violent offending". *Criminology,* 29, 519-529.

Kaplan, H (1980). "Self-esteem and self-derogation theory of drug abuse". *NIDA Research Monograph Service* Mar; 30:128-31. (ADAI bk)

Kelling, G. L., and Coles, C. M. (1996). Fixing Broken Windows: Restoring Order and Reducing Crime in Our Communities, New York: Simon & Schuster.

Kenney, D., and S. Watson (1999). "Crime in the Schools: reducing conflict with problem solving". *National Institute of Justice: Research in Brief.* Washington, DC: National Institute of Justice.

Kline, R. (1998). *Principles and Practice of Structural Equation Modeling.* New York: The Guilford Press.

Klinteberg, B., T. Andersson, D. Magnusson, H. Stattin (1993). "Hyperactive behavior in children as related to subsequent alcohol problems and violent offending: a longitudinal study of male subjects". *Personality Individual Differences.* 15; pp 381-388.

Kohlberg, L. (1958). The Development of Modes of Moral Thinking and Choice in Years Ten to Sixteen. Ph.D. Dissertation: University of Chicago.

Kohlberg, L. (1963). "The development of children's orientations toward a moral order. Sequence of moral thought." *Vita Humana.* 6, pp 11-33.

Kohlberg, L. (1968). "The child as a moral philosopher", *Psychology Today,* 2, pp. 24-31.

Kohlberg, L. (1968). "Moral Development", in *International Encyclopedia of the Social Sciences.* New York: McMillan.

Kohlberg, L. (1969). "Stage and sequence: the cognitive-developmental approach to socialization". In *Handbook of Socialization Theory and Research.* D. Goslin (ed). Chicago: Rand McNally.

Kohlberg, L. (1971). "Cognitive developmental theory and the practice of collective moral education", in M. Wolins and M. Gottesman (eds). *Group Care: The Education Path of Youth Aliyah.*

Kohlberg, L. (1976). "Moral stages and moralization," in T. Likona (ed). *Moral Development and Behavior,* 31-53. New York: Holt, Rinehart, and Winston.

Kohlberg, L. (1981). *Essays on Moral Development: In the Philosophy of Moral Development.* New York: Harper and Row.

Kohlberg, L. (1984). *The Psychology of Moral Development: the Nature and Validity of Moral Stages.* San Francisco: Harper and Row.

Kohlberg, L. (1986). "A current statement on some theoretical issues". In S. Modgil and C. Modgil (eds). *Lawrence Kohlberg: Consensus and Controversy.* London: The Falmer Press.

Kohlberg, L., and E. Turiel (1971). "Moral development and moral education". In G. Lesser (ed) *Psychology and Educational Practice.* Chicago: Scott, Foresman.

Kohlberg, L. and D. Elfenbein. (1975). "The development of moral judgment concerning capital punishment". *American Journal of Orthopsychiatry,* 45, pp. 614-640.

Law-Related Education Evaluation Project (1983). *Social Science Education Consortium.* Boulder, CO: Center for Action Research, 1983.

Law-Related Education Project Exchange (1982). "Two year study indicates that LRE can reduce juvenile delinquency. *LRE Project Exchange,* Winter, 1982.

Lee,V., L.Winfield, and T. Wilson (1991). Academic behaviors among high-achieving African American students. *Education and Urban Society,* 24(1), 65- 86.

Levine, F., and J. Tapp (1977). "The dialectic of legal socialization in community and school". In *Law, Justice, and the Individual in Society: Psychological and Legal Issues.* J. Tapp and F. Levine (eds.). New York: Holt, Rinehart, and Wilson.

Levinson, B. (2001). *We Are All Equal: Student Culture and Identity at a Mexican Secondary School.* Durham: Duke University Press.

LH Research, Inc. (1993). *A survey of experiences, perceptions, and apprehensions about guns among young people in America.* Harvard School of Public Health: Boston.

Lind, A.E., Kray, L., and Thompson, L. (2001). Primacy effects in justice judgments: Testing predictions from fairness heuristic theory. *Organization Behavior & Human Decision Processes*, 85 (2), 189-210.

Lo, T. (1999). "Educating for morality – a report from Hong Kong". http: www.civnet.org/journal/vol3no3/fttwing.htm .

Loeber, R. and Farrington, D.P. (Eds.) (2001).Child Delinquents: Development, Intervention and Service Needs. Thousand Oaks, CA: Sage.

Loesel, F., & T. Biesener. (1990). Resilience in adolescence: A study on the generalizability of protective factors. In: K. Hurrelmann & F. Loesel (Eds.), *Health Hazards in Adolescence*, 299-320. New York: Walter de Gruter.

Luthar, S. S. (1991). Vulnerability and resilience: A study of high risk adolescents. *Child Development,* 62, 600-616.

MacCallum, R., D. Wegener, B. Uchino, and L. Fabrigar (1993). "The problem of equivalent models in applications of covariance structure analysis". *Psychological Bulletin*, 114, 185-199.

Maguin, E., J. Hawkins, R. Catalano, K. Hill, R. Abbott, and T. Herrenkohl. (1995). "Risk factors measured at three ages for violence at age 17-18". Paper presented at the American Society of Criminology, Boston, MA.

Markowitz, A. (1986). "The impact of law-related education on elementary children in reducing delinquent behavior". Unpublished dissertation.

Markwood, J. (1975). "Knowledge and attitudes regarding the juvenile justice system among delinquent and non-delinquent youth". Unpublished dissertation.

Marshall, G. (1977). "Due Process in England". In J. Roland Pennock and John W. Chapman (eds.). *Due Process*. New York: New York University Press.

Matza, D. and Sykes, G., (1957). "Techniques of neutralization: a theory of delinquency". *American Sociological Review,* 22 (December), 665-670.

Mead, G. (1934). *Mind, Self, and Society.* Chicago: University of Chicago Press.

Mendez, J.(1999). "Problems of lawless violence". In *The (Un)Rule of Law*. Notre Dame: University of Notre Dame Press. Pp. 1-19.

Merton, R. (1968). *Social Theory and Social Structure*. New York: Free Press.

McKnight, L. R., & Loper, A. B. (2002). "The effects of risk and resilience factors on the prediction of delinquency in adolescent girls". *School Psychology International*, 23. 186-198.

Minturn, L., and J. Tapp (1970). *Authority, Rules, and Aggression: A cross-national study of children's judgments of the justice of aggressive confrontations: Part II*. Washington, DC: United States Department of Health, Education, and Welfare.

Morash, M. (1978). "Implications of the theory o f legal socialization for understanding the effect of juvenile justice procedures on youths". Unpublished dissertation.

Morash, M. (1983). "An Explanation of Juvenile Delinquency: the integration of moral-reasoning theory and sociological knowledge". *Personality, Moral Development and Criminal Behavior*

Nagin, D. and R. Paternoster. (1991). "The preventive effects of the perceived risk of arrest: testing an expanded conception of delinquency". *Criminology, 29,* 561-85.

National Strategy Information Center (2001). School-Based Education to Counter Crime and Corruption, 3rd Draft.

Nedwek, B. (1987). "Political socialization and policy evaluation: the case of youth employment and training program". *Evaluation and Program Planning,* 10: 35-42.

Nield, R. (2001). "From National Security to Citizen Security: civil society and the evolution of public order debates". Rights and Democracy: International Center for Human Rights and Democratic Development.

Olmstead v. United States. 277 US 438 (1928).

Orlando, L. (2001). *Fighting the Mafia and Renewing Sicilian Culture*. San Francisco: Encounter Books.

Palmer, E. (2003). *Offending Behavior: Moral Reasoning, Criminal Conduct, and the Rehabilitation of Offenders*. Cornwall: Willan Publishing.

Patterson, G., and K.Yoerger. (1993). "Developmental models for delinquent behavior". In *Mental Disorders and Crime.* S. Hodgins (ed.). Newbury Park, CA: Sage.

Palonsky, S., and M. Jacobson. (1982). "The measurement of law-related," *Journal of Social Studies Research,* 6 (1), pp. 22-28.

Piaget, J (1932). *The Moral Judgment of the Child.* New York: Kegan, Paul, Trench, Trubner.

Piaget, J. (1970/1983). "Piaget's Theory," in P.H. Mussen (ed), *Handbook of Child Psychology,* I, 103-128, New York: Wiley.

Pimental, S. (2000). *The nexus of organized crime and politics in Mexico. In Organized Crime and Democratic Accountability.* Eds. J. Bailey and R. Godson. University of Pittsburgh Press. Pittsburg, PA. pp 33-56.

Pinheiro, P. (1999). "The rule of law and the underprivileged in Latin America". In *The (Un)Rule of Law.* Notre Dame: University of Notre Dame Press, pp 1-19.

Portune, R. (1965). "An analysis of attitudes of junior high school pupils toward police officers applied to the preparation of a work of juvenile fiction". Unpublished dissertation.

Pro Juarez, M. (2001). *Legalized Injustice: Mexican Criminal Procedure and Human Rights.* New York: Lawyers Committee for Human Rights.

Radke-Yarrow, M., & Brown, E. (1993). Resilience and vulnerability in children of multiple-risk families. Development and Psychopathology, 5, 581-592.

Rafky , D., and R. Sealey (1975). "The adolescent and the law: a survey". *Crime and Delinquency,* 21, pp. 131-38.

Rawls, J. (1971). *A Theory of Justice.* Cambridge, MA: Harvard University Press.

Reams, B. (in press). "Mexico". *Encyclopedia of International Law Enforcement.* Berkeley: Sage Publications.

Reding, A. (1995). *Democracy and Human Rights in Mexico.* New York: World Policy Institute.

Reiss, A., and J. Roth. (1993). *Understanding and Preventing Violence.* Washington, DC: National Academy Press.

Rengifo, A. (2003). "Internal consistency in cross-cultural research: working with the NSIC Instrument in Baja California, Mexico". Unpublished paper submitted for doctoral course work.

Rest, J. (1979). *Development in Judging Moral Issues.* Minneapolis: University of Minnesota Press.

Rest. J., Narvaez, M. Bebeau, and S. Thoma (1999) *Postconventional Moral Thinking: a neo-Kohlbergian approach.* Lawrence Erlbaum Associates: Mahwah, New Jersey.

Rodley. (1999). Commission on Human Rights Hears Allegations of Violations Against Prisoners, Detainees. United Nations.

Rosenberg, M., Schooler, C., & Schoenback, C. (1989). "Self-esteem and adolescent problems: Modeling reciprocal effects". *American Sociological Review*, 54, 1004-1018.

Rotter, J.B. (1954). *Social Learning and Clinical Psychology.* Prentice Hall: Englewood, Cliffs.

Rutter, M., D. Quinton, and J. Hill (1990). "Adult outcomes of institution-reared children: males and females compared." In Lee Robins and Michael Rutter (eds.), *Straight and Devious Pathways from Childhood to Adulthood.* Cambridge: Cambridge University Press.

Rutter, M. (1987). Psychosocial resilience and protective mechanisms. *American Journal of Orthopsychiatry* 57, 316-331.

Sampson, R. and J. Laub. (1993). *Crime in the Making: Pathways and Turning Points Throughout Life.* Harvard University Press.

Sampson, R., S. Raudenbush, and F. Earls (1997). "Neighborhoods and violent crime: a multi-level study of collective efficacy". *Science, 277,* 918-924.

Schneider, J. (1998). "Educating against the Mafia: a report from Sicily". http://www.civnet.org/journal/issue5/ftjschn.htm.

Serious Habitual Offender Comprehensive Action Program (1998). Washington, DC: Office of Juvenile Justice and Delinquency Prevention.

Sedikides, A. (1989). "Relations between role-taking opportunities and moral judgment development". Ohio State University: unpublished dissertation.

Shadish, W., T. Cook, and D. Campbell. (2002). *Experimental and Quasi-Experimental Designs for Generalized Causal Inference.* Houghton Mifflin Company: Boston, MA.

Sheppard, D., H. Grant, and W. Rowe. (1999). "Fighting Gun Violence". *OJJDP Bulletin in Brief.* Washington, DC: Office of Juvenile Justice and Delinquency Prevention.

Sheppard, D., P. Kelly, and H. Grant (2001). "Juvenile Gun Courts". *JAIBG Bulletin.* Washington, DC: Office of Juvenile Justice and Delinquency Prevention.

Sugawara, H. and R. MacCullum (1993). "Effect of estimation method on incremental fit indexes for covariance structure models". *Applied Psychological Measurement,* 17, 365-377.

Sieb, L., and W. Schmoll. (1985). "Using law-related education to reduce juvenile delinquency". *The Police Chief,* January 1985, pp. 39-41.

Simpson, E.L. (1974). "Moral development research: a case study of scientific cultural bias". *Human Development,* 17, 81-106.

Singer, M., T. Anglin, L. Song, and L. Lunghofer (1995). "Adolescents' exposure to violence and associated symptoms of psychological trauma". *Journal of the American Medical Association,* 273, 477-482.

Snarey, J. (1985). "The cross-cultural universality of socio-moral development: a review of Kohlbergian research". *Psychological Bulletin,* 97, 202-32.

Sutherland, E. (1947). *Principles of Criminology,* (4th ed.), Philadelphia: J.B. Lippincott.

Sutherland, E. (1978). *Criminology.* (10th ed.), Philadelphia: J.B. Lippincott.

Tapp, J.L. (1970). "What rule? What role?" *U.C.L.A Law Review,* 17 (6), 1333-1344.

Tapp, J.L., and L. Kohlberg (1971). "Developing senses of law and legal justice", *Journal of Social Issues,* 27 (2), 65-91.

Tapp, J.L. (1987). "Legal socialization across age, culture, and context: psychological considerations for children and adults in the criminal and legal justice systems". Rutgers University.

Tapp, J.L. and Levine F. (1974). "Legal socialization: strategies for an ethical legality". *Stanford Law Review,* 21 (1). Leland Stanford Junior University.

Tapp, J.L. and Levine, F. (1977). *Law, justice, and the individual in society: psychological and legal issues.* New York: Holt, Rinehart and Winston.

Tapp, J.L., and L. Kohlberg (1977). "Developing senses of law and legal justice". In J.L Tapp and F.J. Levine (eds.). *Law, justice, and the individual in society.* New York: Holt, Rinehart, and Winston.

Thornberry, T. (1994). *Violent families and youth violence.* Washington, DC: National Institute of Justice.

Tiet QQ, Bird HR, Davies M, et al (1998). "Adverse life events and resilience". *Journal of American Academy of Child Adolescent Psychiatry,* 1998; 37 :1191 –1200.

Tiet, Q. Q., & Huizinga, D. (2002). Dimensions of the construct of resilience and adaptation among inner city youth. Journal of Adolescent Research, 17, 260-276.

Turiel, E. (1997). "The development of morality." In William Damon and Nancy Eisenberg, ed. *Handbook of Child Psychology,* Volume 3, Social, Emotional, and Personality Development, 5th Edition. New York: Wiley, 863-932.

Tyler, T (1990). *Why People Obey the Law.* New Haven, CT: Yale University Press.

Tyler, T. and K. Rasinski (1991). "Procedural justice, institutional legitimacy, and the acceptance of unpopular U.S. Supreme Court decisions: a reply to Gibson". *Law and Society Review,* 25, 621.

Tyler, T. (2000). "Multiculturalism and the willingness of citizens to defer to law and legal authorities". *Law and Social Inquiry,* 25, (4), 983-1019.

Tyler, T., and C. Lind (1992). "A relational model of authority in groups". *Advances in Experimental Social Psychology,* 25, New York: Academic Press.

Wallerstein J. S, & Kelly J. B (1980). *Surviving The Breakup: How Children and Parents Cope With Divorce.* Basic Books: New York.

Wallerstein, J., & Kelly, J. (1979). Children and divorce: a review. *Social Work*, 24(6), 468-475.

Wells, E., & Rankin, J. (1983). Self concept as a mediating factor in delinquency. *Social Psychology Quarterly*, 46, 11-22.

Werner, E.E. (1984). "Resilient children". *Young Children*, 40, 68-72.

Werner, E. (1994). "Overcoming the odds". *Developmental and Behavioral Pediatrics*, 15, 131-136.

Wiatrowski, M., and A. Pritchard. (2003). "Democratic Policing, Post Conflict Criminology, and Democratic Development". Unpublished Paper presented at the American Society of Criminology Conference in Denver, Colorado: November, 2003.

Wilson, James Q. and Herrnstein, Richard (1986). *Crime and Human Nature: The Definitive Study of the Causes of Crime*. New York: Simon and Schuster.

Wilson, J., and G. Kelling (1982). "The police and neighborhood safety". *The Atlantic* (March 1982): 29-38.

Wood, A. (2001). "Palermo Creates a Culture of Legality; Economic Growth Follows".Wysiwyg://16/http://www.businessjournal.com/SICILYTO UR/Palermo.htm.

Worden, R. (1995). "The Causes of Police Brutality: theory and evidence on police use of force". In *And Justice For All: Understanding and Controlling Police Abuse of Force*. William Geller and Hans Toch (eds.), pp. 31-60. Washington, DC: Police Executive Research Forum.

Zimmer, J. and S. Huston (1987). "Law-related education: an Iowa success story". *Corrections Today*, October 1987, pp.16-20.

Zvekic, U (1998). "Policing and attitudes towards the police in countries in transition: preliminary results of the International Crime (Victim) Survey". *Policing and Society*, Vol 8, pp. 205-224.

INDEX